KANJI
de MANGA
Vol. 6

MANGA UNIVERSITY presents...

The Comic Book That Teaches You How To Read And Write Japanese!

volume 6

Created by Glenn Kardy   Art by Chihiro Hattori

Japanime

TOKYO   SAN FRANCISCO

Manga University Presents ... Kanji de Manga
The Comic Book That Teaches You
How To Read And Write Japanese
Volume Six

Published by Manga University under the auspices of Japanime Co. Ltd.,
3-31-18 Nishi-Kawaguchi, Kawaguchi-shi, Saitama-ken 332–0021, Japan.

www.mangauniversity.com

First edition, September 2008

ISBN-13: 978-4-921205-11-9
ISBN-10: 4-921205-11-6

07 08 09 10   10 9 8 7 6 5 4 3 2 1

Printed in Canada

CONTENTS

The Manga University Mission Statement

The mission of Manga University is to enlighten and educate the international community on all aspects of Japanese culture through the creative use of traditional manga artwork.

The university recognizes that manga transcends mainstream entertainment and possesses a unique ability to convey the true spirit of Japan, making the art form an ideal communicative tool to touch the lives and inspire the minds of Japan enthusiasts worldwide.

Our mission and philosophy are firmly rooted in the principles and conviction of the Japanese educational tradition and in the best ideals of Japanese heritage.

Founded at the turn of the century and located in Tokyo, Manga University is one of the world's foremost publishers of manga-themed educational materials.

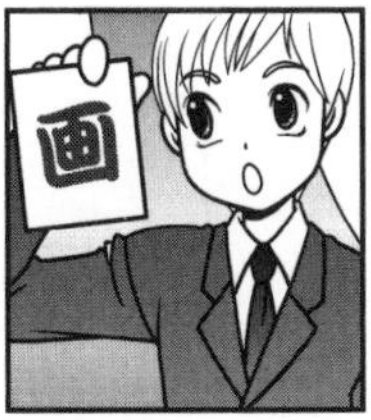
画

INTRODUCTION

Looking back is not something we usually do when we learn. Usually, we're too focused on the next challenge waiting to be conquered, that next set of formidable kanji, so there's no time to stop and reflect.

But take a moment now and look through this book. Of course, most of what you'll see in the following pages will be unfamiliar. After all, these are new kanji to you and you're here to learn them.

And this is where, for a brief moment, we are going to pause and take that look back.

Think of the very first time you cracked open your first volume of *Kanji de Manga*. If you're a true Japanophile or manga maniac, you probably skimmed through the pages to see the words you would be learning and check out the great manga art. And that's probably when it hit you, maybe for the first time, just how hard this would be. Not only were the kanji totally unfamiliar, but many of the basic radicals were new and alien as well. Maybe, at that moment, the task seemed overwhelming, even frightening.

Maybe you even began to wonder just what you had gotten yourself into.

We've tried to make it as easy as possible, but there is no denying it: Japanese is a hard language for nonnatives to learn to speak, and an even harder one to learn to write. Although each kanji in that first volume featured some of the common compounds it could form, our focus then was simply learning the characters themselves and the kanji basics. Forming your own compounds probably seemed a long way off.

But look at where you are today!

You now have several hundred kanji under your belt. You've conquered many of the most basic and crucial characters for everyday Japanese reading and writing. You can start to write compounds and even full sentences of your own. You can probably even pick up a Japanese newspaper, and while you may not be able to read it fluently, you can certainly understand it well enough to get a sense of what's going on. And that's before you start on this volume and add dozens more to your already formidable repertoire.

When you are done with this book, you will be making good time on the road to literacy in one of the world's most challenging languages.

はじめましょう！

PAGE GUIDE

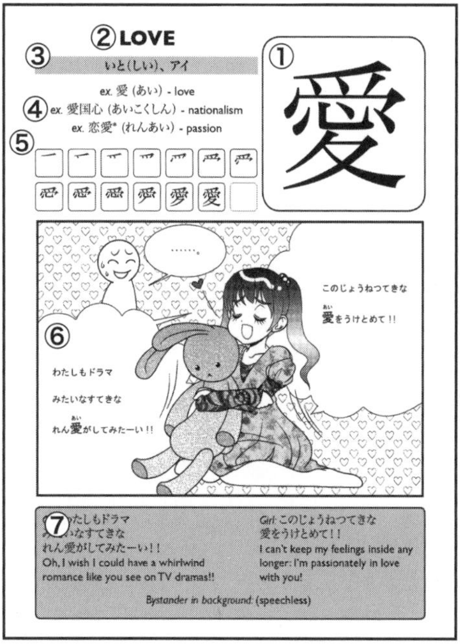

②LOVE
③
いと(しい)、アイ
ex. 愛 (あい) - love
④ex. 愛国心 (あいこくしん) - nationalism
ex. 恋愛* (れんあい) - passion
⑤
①
愛
……。
このじょうねつてきな
愛をうけとめて!!
⑥
わたしもドラマ
みたいなすてきな
れん愛がしてみたーい!!
⑦
たしもドラマ
いなすてきな
れん愛がしてみたーい!!
Oh, I wish I could have a whirlwind romance like you see on TV dramas!!
Girl: このじょうねつてきな
愛をうけとめて!!
I can't keep my feelings inside any longer: I'm passionately in love with you!
Bystander in background: (speechless)

① The featured kanji

② Common definition

③ Readings: kun-yomi (Japanese readings) are written in hiragana, while on-yomi (Chinese readings) are in katakana.

④ Examples of compounds containing the featured kanji, their pronunciations (written in hiragana) and English definitions. (An asterisk next to a compound indicates that one or more of its kanji are not featured in this or any of the previous volumes of the "Kanji de Manga" series.)

⑤ Stroke order: In general, the strokes are written from top to bottom and left to right. For a list of additional stroke-order rules, please refer to the chart at the back of this book.

⑥ The manga. All dialogue is written in hiragana and katakana except for the single featured kanji. The proper pronunciation of the kanji is indicated in furigana (tiny hiragana) written above the character.

⑦ Translation of the dialogue and selected onomatopoeia.

Kanji de Manga

そわ
さっそく
はじめましょう！

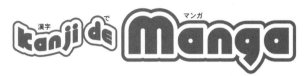

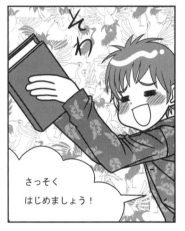

STUDY SECTION

遊

PLAY

あそ(ぶ)、ユウ

ex. 遊ぶ (あそぶ) - to play
ex. 遊戯* (ゆうぎ) - game
ex. 遊具 (ゆうぐ) - playground equipment

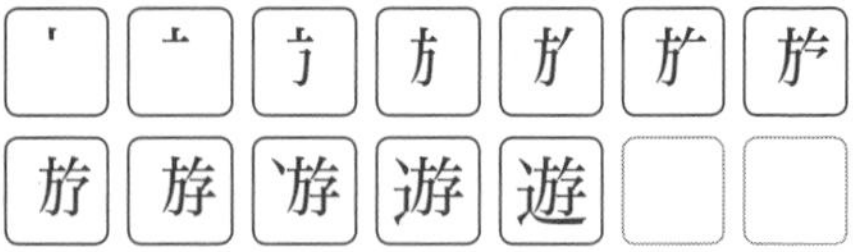

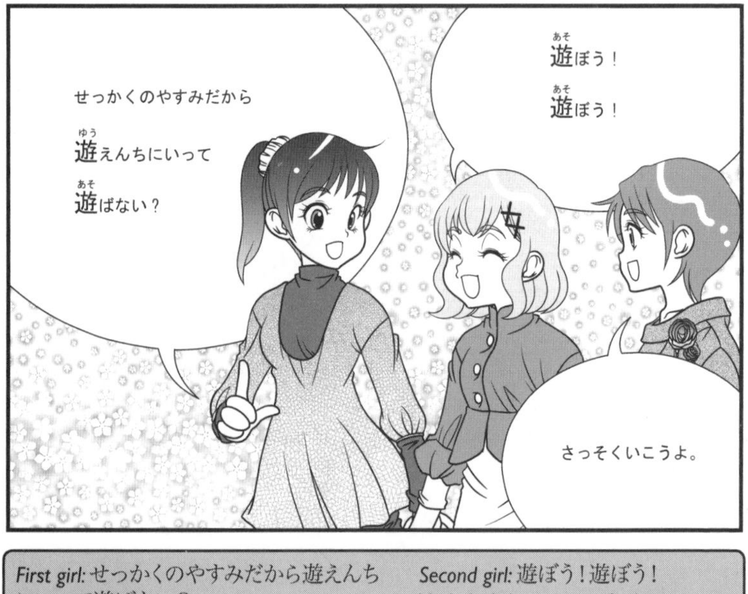
せっかくのやすみだから 遊(ゆう)えんちにいって 遊(あそ)ばない？
遊(あそ)ぼう！ 遊(あそ)ぼう！
さっそくいこうよ。

First girl: せっかくのやすみだから遊えんちにいって遊ばない？
Since we're finally on vacation, why don't we go hang out at the amusement park?

Second girl: 遊ぼう！遊ぼう！
Yeah, let's have some fun!

Third girl: さっそくいこうよ。
All right, let's go!

OIL / FAT

油

あぶら、ユ

ex. 油 (あぶら) - oil
ex. 油絵 (あぶらえ) - oil painting
ex. 油分 (ゆぶん) - oil content

ついつい油(あぶら)っこいもの
ばかりたべちゃった…。
さいきん油(ゆ)ぶんの
とりすぎだよなぁ・・・。
……。
ぷよっ

Boy: ついつい油っこいもの ばかりたべちゃった・・・。
I just can't stop myself from eating really oily foods...

さいきん油ぶんのとりすぎだよなぁ・・・。
I think maybe I've been taking in too much fat lately.

ぷよっ (jiggling)

Girl: (speechless)

REFORM

ex. 改める (あらためる) - to reform; to revise
ex. 改心 (かいしん) - reform (of the heart)
ex. 改造* (かいぞう) - modification

改ぞうに
改ぞうをかさね・・・

きょうここに
かんせい！！

１ごう改め２ごう！！！

どーん

うわー！！
すごーい！！

Older brother: 改ぞうに
改ぞうをかさね・・・
After customizing all of my
modifications...
きょうここにかんせい！！
Today, at this very moment, it's
finally complete!

Older brother: １ごう改め２ごう！！！
Version 1 is now version 2!!!
どーん (ta-da!)
Younger brother: うわー！！すごーい！！
Whoa!! That's awesome!!

PLAN

アン

ex. 案 (あん) - plan
ex. 案内 (あんない) - instructions
ex. 思案中 (しあんちゅう) - in thought

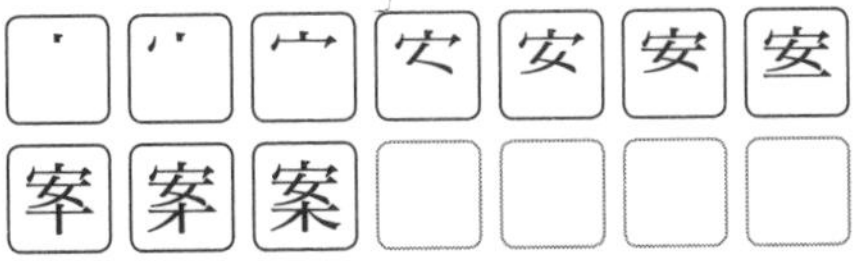

`	` `	⼧	⼧	安	安	安
宰	宰	案				

ほかになにか
案のあるひとは？

し案ちゅう・・・。

あのー・・・
こんな案は
どうですか？

なかなか
これはいい案かも
しれないな。

First boy: ほかになにか案のあるひとは？
Has anyone come up with any other proposals?

Second boy: し案ちゅう・・・。
I'm still thinking...

Girl: あのー・・・こんな案はどうですか？
Umm... How about this idea?

First boy: なかなかこれはいい案かもしれないな。
You know, this might be a really good plan.

委

COMMITTEE

イ

ex. 委員会 (いいんかい) - committee meeting
ex. 委託* (いたく) - entrust
ex. 委任状* (いにんじょう) - permission slip

じかいの委いんかいは らいしゅう かいさいします。
ぺらっ
しゅっせきできないひとは、 この委にんじょうに クラス、しめい、りゆう をかいてあすまでに、 ていしゅつしてください。
ハ
イ

Student body president: じかいの委いんかいはらいしゅうかいさいします。
Our next committee meeting will be held next week.

ぺらっ (flapping a piece of paper)

しゅっせきできないひとは、この委にんじょうにクラス、しめい、りゆうをかいてあすまでに、ていしゅつしてください。 Those who can't attend must fill out this absence form with their class, position and reason and hand it in by tomorrow.
Students (in unison): ハーイ OK!

STOMACH

胃

イ

ex. 胃 (い) - stomach

ex. 胃潰瘍* (いかいよう) - stomach ulcer

ex. 胃薬 (いぐすり) - stomach medicine

どうも胃のちょうしが
わるいみたいなんだ。
キリキリキリ
だいじょうぶ？
胃ぐすりをのめば
おさまるのだけどね・・・。
たいへんね。
キリキリ
キリ

Brother: どうも胃のちょうしが
わるいみたいなんだ。
For some reason my stomach seems to be disagreeing with me.

キリキリキリ (stomach pains)

Sister: だいじょうぶ？ Are you OK?

Brother: 胃ぐすりをのめば
おさまるのだけどね・・・。
I think I'll feel better if I take some stomach medicine...

Sister: たいへんね。
It must feel awful.

板

BOARD / PLATE

いた、ハン、バン

ex. 板 (いた) - board
ex. 板前 (いたまえ) - chef; cook
ex. 看板 (かんばん) - sign

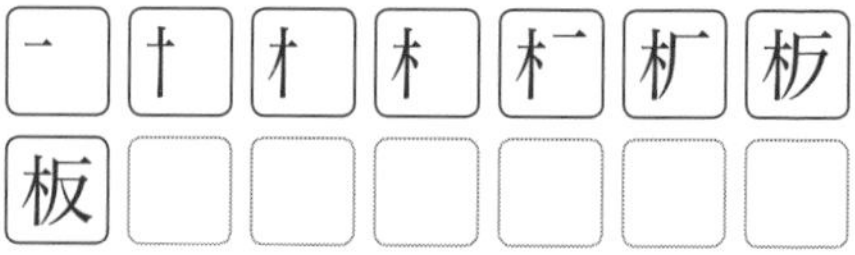

おおきな板をもっているけど なにかするの？
ぶんかさいでつかう かん板をつくるんだ。
たのしみだよね。

Girl: おおきな板をもっているけど なにかするの？
What are you doing with that giant board?

Boy: ぶんかさいでつかうかん板をつくるんだ。
I'm using it to make a sign for the school cultural festival.

Girl: たのしみだよね。
Sounds like fun.

LOVE

いと（しい）、アイ

ex. 愛 (あい) - love
ex. 愛国心 (あいこくしん) - nationalism
ex. 恋愛* (れんあい) - passion

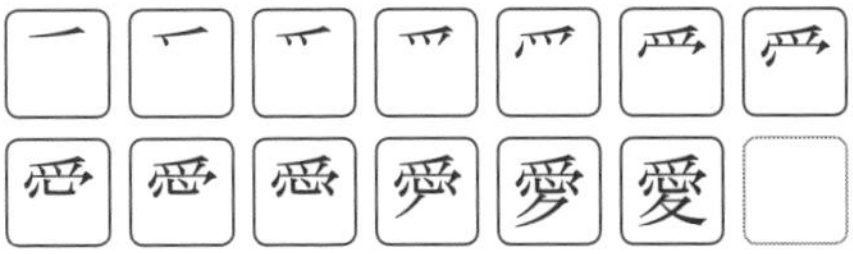

このじょうねつてきな
愛<ruby>あい</ruby>をうけとめて！！

わたしもドラマ

みたいなすてきな

れん愛<ruby>あい</ruby>がしてみたーい！！

Girl: わたしもドラマ
みたいなすてきな
れん愛がしてみたーい！！
Oh, I wish I could have a whirlwind
romance like you see on TV dramas!!

Girl: このじょうねつてきな
愛をうけとめて！！
I can't keep my feelings inside any
longer: I'm passionately in love
with you!

Bystander in background: (speechless)

FATE

いのち、メイ、ミョウ

ex. 命拾い (いのちびろい) - evade death
ex. 救命* (きゅうめい) - lifesaving
ex. 生命力 (せいめいりょく) - vitality

ノ　人　一　个　仐　슶　命
命

きゅう**命**ボートで
はつかかんひょうりゅうして
たすかった！？

すごいせい**命**りょく・・・
よく**命**びろいしたなぁ。
でも、たすかってよかった。

Student: きゅう命ボートではつ
かかんひょうりゅうしてたすかった！？
A lifeboat was rescued after
being adrift for 20 days!?

ばさっ (throwing open the
newspaper)

すごいせい命りょく・・・
よく命びろいしたなぁ。
でも、たすかってよかった。
Wow, that's amazing resilience in
the face of death. I'm so glad they
were saved.

CHASE / FOLLOW

お(う)、ツイ

ex. 追う (おう) - to follow
ex. 追加 (ついか) - an addition
ex. 追跡* (ついせき) - pursuit

はんにんがにげたぞー！！

はんにんをにがすな！！

追え！！
追うんだー！！！

ちょっと追せき
するにんずう
おおすぎじゃねーか！？

Cop: はんにんがにげたぞー！！
That criminal is getting away!!
はんにんをにがすな！！
Don't let him escape!!
くわっ (pointing)
追え！！追うんだー！！！
Chase him!! After him!!!

ドドドドドド (running)

Criminal: ちょっと追せきするにんずう
おおすぎじゃねーか！？
Isn't that just a few too many people
coming to get me!?

億

HUNDRED MILLION

オク

ex. 一億円 (いちおくえん) - ¥100,000,000

ex. 億万長者 (おくまんちょうじゃ) - billionaire

ex. 巨億* (きょおく) - vast fortune

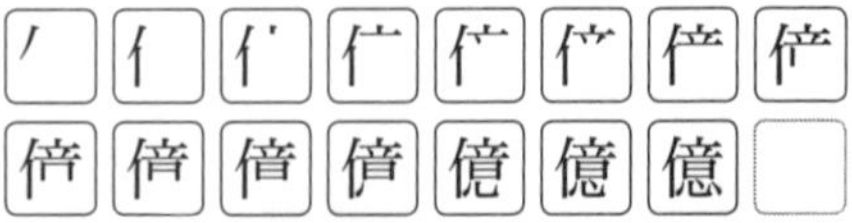

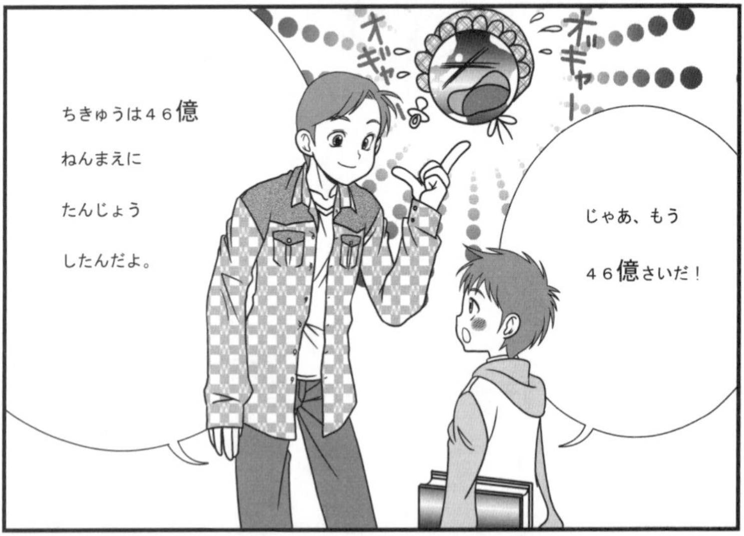
ちきゅうは４６億
ねんまえに
たんじょう
したんだよ。
オギャー
オギャー
じゃあ、もう
４６億さいだ！

Father: ちきゅうは46億ねんまえにたんじょうしたんだよ。
Did you know, the earth was born forty six hundred million years ago.

オギャーオギャー (baby crying)

Son: じゃあ、もう46億さいだ！
Well then, that would make it a forty six hundred million-year-old!

FALL / DROP

お(ちる)、お(とす)、ラク

ex. 落ち込む* (おちこむ) - to be down
ex. 落選 (らくせん) - rejection
ex. 落胆* (らくたん) - discouragement

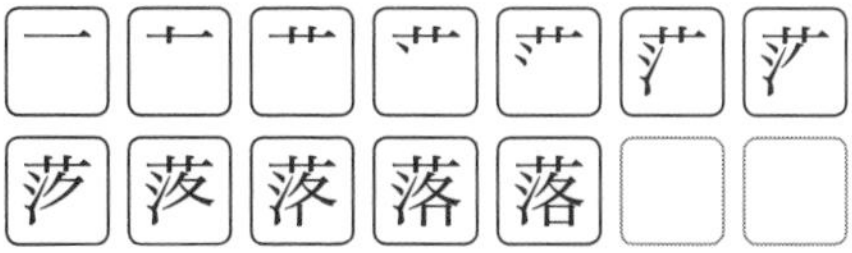

一	十	�艹	⺭	汁	汁	芗
芗	茨	落	落	落		

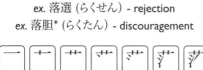

わ!!
すごい落たんぶり!

どよーーん

オーディションに落せん
しちゃったー!!

そんなに落ちこまないで!
つぎのチャンスを
がんばって。

めそ

めそ

Big sister: わ！！す
ごい落たんぶり！
**Gah!! She looks so
dejected!**

どよ〜ん (disappointment)

Little sister: オーディションに落せん
しちゃったー！！！ **I didn't make the audition!!**
ぴー (crying)
Big sister: そんなに落ちこまないで！つぎのチャン
スをがんばって。**Don't let it get you so down!
Just do your best the next chance you get.**
めそめそ (tears welling up)

各

EACH

おのおの、カク

ex. 各 (かく) - each
ex. 各自 (かくじ) - each individual
ex. 各種* (かくしゅ) - all kinds

ノ ク 夂 夂 各 各

はーい、
各じはんにわかれてさぎょうを
はじめてー。
ぱんぱん

各はんのはんちょうは、さぎょう
しゅうりょうご
各こうもくをうめた
このようしをていしゅつしてね。

Teacher: はーい、各じはんにわかれてさぎょうをはじめてー。
All right, I'd like you all to separate and begin work.
ぱんぱん (clapping for attention)

各はんのはんちょうは、さぎょうしゅうりょうご各こうもくをうめたこのようしをていしゅつしてね。
And I'd like the head of each group to fill in each item on this form and then turn it in.

REMEMBER

覚

おぼ(える)、さ(ます)、カク

ex. 覚える (おぼえる) - to remember
ex. 自覚 (じかく) - self-consciousness
ex. 目が覚める (めがさめる) - to wake up

ふあああああ…
のび〜
あ、
めが覚めた？
あれ・・・？
ねてた・・・？
ええ!!
覚えていないの !?
しょくじをしてすぐ
ねちゃったのよ！
そのへんじ覚
してよね。
ごめんなさい・・・。

ふあああああ・・・ (yawning)

Mother: あ、めが覚めた？ Oh, you're awake?

のび〜 (stretching)

Son: あれ・・・？ねてた・・・？ Huh...? Was I asleep...?

Mother: ええ！！覚えていないの！？ What!! You don't remember!? しょくじをしてすぐねちゃったのよ！そのへんじ覚してよね。You ate and fell right asleep! You should pay attention to things like that.

Son: ごめんなさい・・・。I'm sorry...

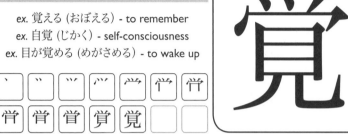

FACE

おも、おもて、つら、めん

ex. 仮面* (かめん) - mask
ex. 面識* (めんしき) - acquaintance
ex. 面接* (めんせつ) - interview

お？

あれ？

ふたりとも

面
めん
しきあったんだ。

いぜん面
めん
せつ

かいじょうで

あったことが

あるんだ。

そうだったんだ。

First boy: お？ Oh?	*Girl:* ふたりとも面しきあったんだ。 I see you two have met before.
Second boy: あれ？ Wha-?	*Second boy:* いぜん面せつかいじょうであったこと があるんだ。 We met before at an interview assembly.
	Girl: そうだったんだ。Oh, I see.

FREIGHT

カ

ex. 貨物列車 (かもつれっしゃ) - freight train
ex. 金貨 (きんか) - coin
ex. 雑貨* (ざっか) - goods; wares

みてみて！
このざっ貨かわいいよ。

ほんとうだ。

きてきて！
こっちの貨もつれっしゃの
もけいもかわいいよ。

ようするに・・・
なんでもかわいいのね。

First girl: みてみて！
このざっ貨かわいいよ。
Look, look! This stuff is really cute.

Second girl: ほんとうだ。
Oh yeah, sure is.

First girl: きてきて！こっちの貨もつれっしゃの
もけいもかわいいよ。C'mere, c'mere! This
model freight train is cute too!

Second girl: ようするに・・・なんでもかわいい
のね。At the end of the day ... just about
anyting is cute to you, huh?

課

CHAPTER / LESSON

カ

ex. 課題曲 (かだいきょく) - set piece of music
ex. 学課 (がっか) - school lesson
ex. 放課後 (ほうかご) - after school

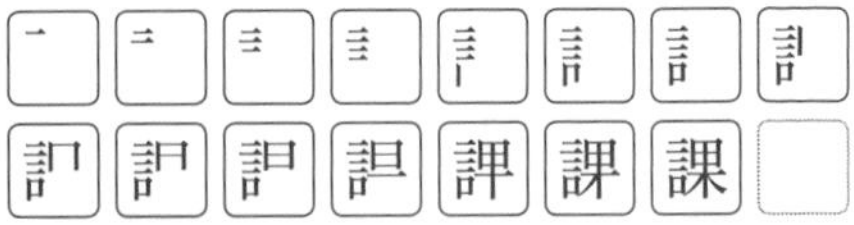

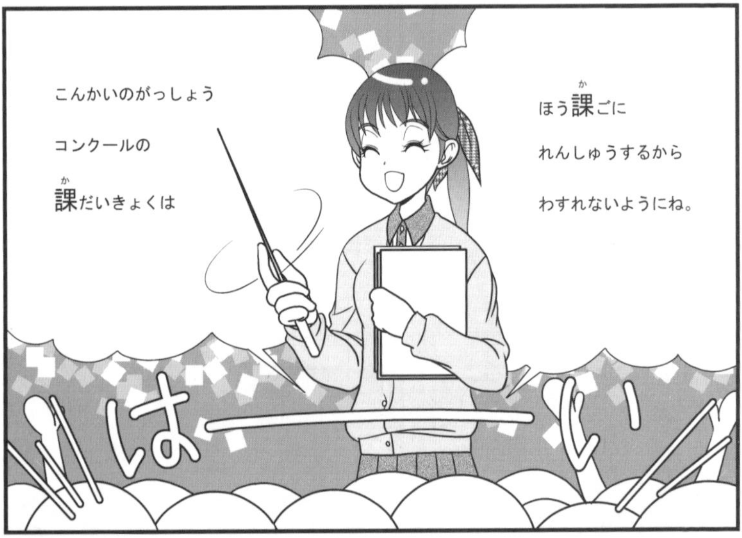
こんかいのがっしょう
コンクールの
課(か)だいきょくは
ほう課(か)ごに
れんしゅうするから
わすれないようにね。
はーい

Choir director: こんかいのがっしょうコンクールの課だいきょくは
ほう課ごにれんしゅうするからわすれないようにね。
The piece of music chosen for our choir competition
will be rehearsed after school, so don't forget to come.

Students (in unison): はーい OK!

MACHINE

カイ

ex. 機械* (きかい) - machine
ex. 器械* (きかい) - appliance
ex. 機械化* (きかいか) - mechanization

なにげなくまいにち
つかっている
けいたいでんわも・・・

すばらしい
せいみつき械
だよな。

College student: なにげなくまいにちつかっているけいたいでんわも・・・
すばらしいせいみつき械だよな。
I use this cell phone every day without really thinking about it...
but it really is an amazing piece of precision machinery.

害

HARM

ガイ

ex. 害 (がい) - injury; harm

ex. 害虫 (がいちゅう) - harmful insect

ex. 妨害* (ぼうがい) - interference

みーん
みん
みーん
せみのこえに害はないけど・・・。
ここまでくると・・・
しずけさをぼう害されてたいへんだよね。
みーん
みーん
みん
みーん
みん
みーん
みーん
みーん
みーん
みーん
げっそり

みーんみーん (the loud chirping of cicadas)

First boy: せみのこえに害はないけど・・・。
It's not like the cicadas' chirping is painful to hear, but...

げっそり (exhausted)

Second boy: ここまでくると・・・
When they get this loud...

しずけさをぼう害されてたいへんだよね。
...it starts to interfere with the peace and quiet.

RETURN

返

かえ(す)、かえ(る)、ヘン

ex. 返す (かえす) - to return (something)
ex. 返事 (へんじ) - response
ex. 返品 (へんぴん) - exchange (goods)

一	厂	万	反	丶反	laboratory	返

おかあさーん！
おおきなカエルをいけで
つかまえたよ！！
!!
いますぐ返(かえ)してきなさい！！
返(へん)じは！？
はーい・・・。
ちぇっ

Boy: おかあさーん！おおきなカエルをいけでつかまえたよ！！
Mom! I caught this big frog down at the lake!!

Mom: いますぐ返してきなさい！！返じは！？
You take that thing back right this minute!! Well? What do you say!?

Boy: はーい・・・。OK...

ちぇっ ("Darn!")

囲

SURROUND

かこ(う)、かこ(む)、イ

ex. 囲む (かこむ) - to surround
ex. 囲碁* (いご) - Go (Japanese board game)
ex. 周囲* (しゅうい) - surroundings

きぎに囲まれていて しずかだね。
しゅう囲のおとなんか きにならないね。

Office worker taking a break in the park: きぎに囲まれていて しずかだね。
It sure is quiet surrounded by all these trees.

Co-worker: しゅう囲のおとなんか きにならないね。
There's no atmospheric noise to bother us.

COMPLETE

カン

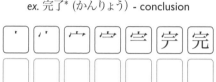

ex. 完結編* (かんけつへん) - last volume
ex. 完全 (かんぜん) - completeness
ex. 完了* (かんりょう) - conclusion

完

そわ
さしえも完ぜんさいげんだし、
よむのがたのしみ。
ついに完けつへんの
ほんがでたぞー。
そわ
そわ

Boy: ついに完けつへんのほんがでたぞー。
The last volume is finally out!
そわそわ (can't sit still)
さしえも完ぜんさいげんだし、よむのがたのしみ。
Even the illustrations have been faithfully reproduced, I'm looking forward to reading this!

GOVERNMENT

カン

ex. 官庁* (かんちょう) - government office
ex. 警察官* (けいさつかん) - police officer
ex. 裁判官* (さいばんかん) - judge

`	´	宀	宀	官	官	官
官						

わたし、
しょうらいきょうしになりたいの。

そうなんだ。

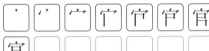

ぼくは
けいさつ官になりたいんだ。

かっこいいー。

Girl: わたし、しょうらいきょうしに
なりたいの。
I'd like to be a teacher when I
grow up.

Boy: そうなんだ。
You don't say.

Boy: ぼくはけいさつ官になりたいんだ。
Well, I wanna become a police officer.

ビシッ (salute)

Girl: かっこいいー。
Cool!

EMOTION

カン

ex. 感じる (かんじる) - to feel
ex. 感情* (かんじょう) - emotion; feeling
ex. 感性* (かんせい) - sensitivity

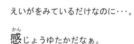

えいがをみているだけなのに・・・。

感(かん)じょうゆたかだなぁ。

感(かん)せいのちがいかしら。

みていてたのしいけど・・・。

Girlfriend: えいがをみているだけなのに・・・。感じょうゆたかだなぁ。
感せいのちがいかしら。みていてたのしいけど・・・。
Even though it's just a movie... he's shows such a range of emotions.
Maybe he's just sensitive. It's actually kind of fun to watch, but...

フー・・・ (sigh)

MEDICINE

くすり、ヤク

ex. 薬 (くすり) - medicine
ex. 薬局 (やっきょく) - pharmacy
ex. 薬指 (くすりゆび) - ring finger

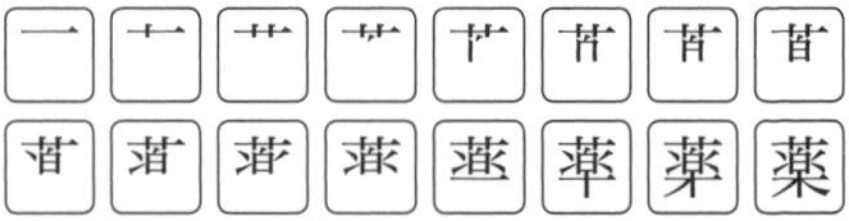

一 十 十 艹 艹 艹 甘 甘

甘 甘 芦 茈 茈 蓮 薬 薬

けっこうアレルギー薬
をきらしているな…。

薬きょくで
しょほうの薬
をほきゅう
しておこう。

Young man: けっこうアレルギー薬を
きらしているな…。
It looks like I'm starting to run low
on my allergy medicine.

薬きょくでしょほうの薬をほきゅう
しておこう。
I better go to the pharmacy and refill my
prescription.

Sign: 薬 (medicine)

(Most pharmacies and drugstores in Japan have large signs that prominently feature the kanji 薬.)

PIPE / TUBE

管

くだ、カン

ex. 木管楽器* (もっかんがっき) - woodwind
ex. 管理 (かんり) - management
ex. 保管* (ほかん) - custody

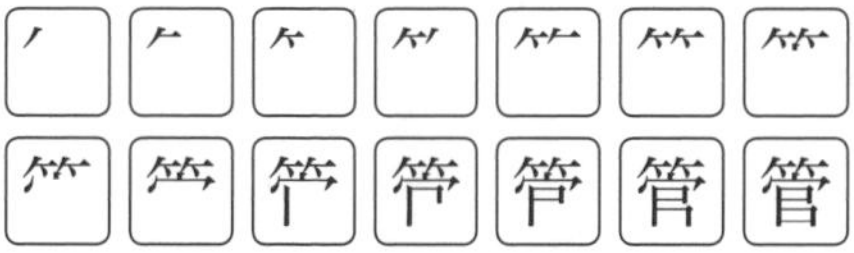

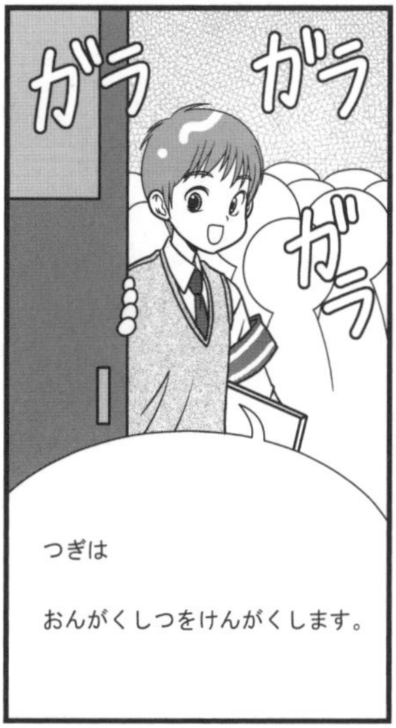
ガラ ガラ
ガラ
つぎは
おんがくしつをけんがくします。

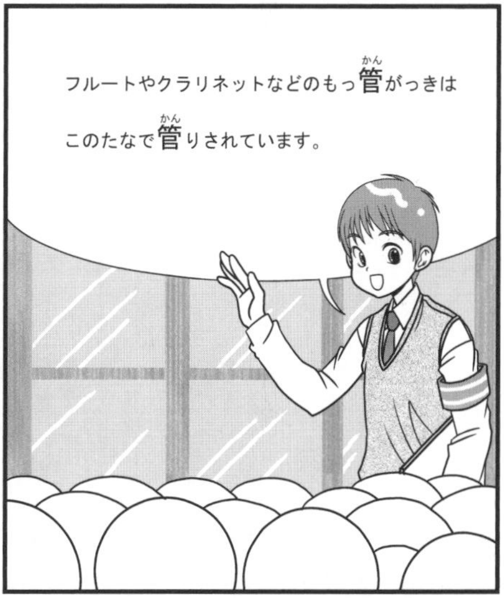
フルートやクラリネットなどのもっ管がっきは
このたなで管りされています。

ガラガラガラ (crowd shuffling)

Tour guide: つぎはおんがくしつをけんがくします。
Next, I'll be giving you a tour of the music room.

フルートやクラリネットなどのもっ管がっきはこのたなで管りされています。
Flutes, clarinets and other woodwind instruments are maintained on this shelf.

配

DISTRIBUTE

くば(る)、ハイ

ex. 配る (くばる) - distribute; hand out
ex. 宅配* (たくはい) - home delivery
ex. 配達* (はいたつ) - delivery

しんぶん配(はい)たつのそうちょうバイトはじめてからねむいよ～・・・。
がんばってるわね。
でも、たいちょうにもきを配(くば)らないとからだこわすよ。
ありがとう。
むりは きんもつだね。

Paperboy: しんぶん配たつのそうちょうバイトはじめてからねむいよ～・・・。
Ever since I've started delivering papers in the morning I've been so tired...
Girl: がんばってるわね。
You must be working pretty hard.

Girl: でも、たいちょうにもきを配らないとからだこわすよ。
But if you don't give enough attention to your body, you'll hurt yourself!
Paperboy: ありがとう。Thanks.
むりはきんもつだね。I'll try not to push it.

RANK/POSITION

くらい、ぐらい、イ

ex. 位地 (いち) - location
ex. 位 (くらい／ぐらい) - about; around
ex. 順位* (じゅんい) - rank

くらい
どの**位**のぼって
きたのかなぁ。

ちずで
かくにんして
みたら？

ちずだとだいたい
い
この**位**ちになるかな。

くらい
はんぶん**位**
のぼってきたのね。

First hiker: どの位のぼってきた
のかなぁ。
I wonder how far we've climbed so far.

Second hiker: ちずでかくにんして
みたら？
How about we check the map?

First hiker: ちずだとだいたいこの位ち
になるかな。According to the map we
should be right around this location.

Second hiker: はんぶん位
のぼってきたのね。
So we've climbed about halfway there.

ADD

くわ(える)、くわ(わる)、カ

ex. 加速 (かそく) - acceleration
ex. 加える (くわえる) - to add
ex. 参加* (さんか) - participation

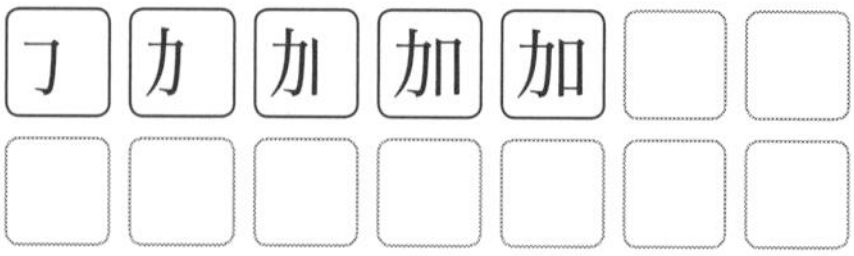

| フ | カ | カ | 加 | 加 | | |

ぼくもメンバーに加えて

もらっていい？

いいけど、ボランティア

かつどうにきょうみ

あったっけ？

これからはためになることに

さん加しなくちゃとおもってね。

さん加

だいかんげいよ。

Student: ぼくもメンバーに加えて
もらっていい？ Could you add me as
a member?

Teacher: いいけど、ボランティア
かつどうにきょうみあったっけ？
Sure, but are you really interested in
doing volunteer work?

Student: これからはためになることに
さん加しなくちゃとおもってね。
I've been thinking it would be good
to get involved.

Teacher: さん加だいかんげいよ。
Well then, you're welcome to join.

CLOTHES

ころも、イ

ex. 衣装* (いしょう) - outfit
ex. 衣類 (いるい) - clothing
ex. 衣替え* (ころもがえ) - switching uniforms

はやく衣（ころも）がえに
ならないかな・・・。

ふだんの衣（い）るいだけじゃなくて
せいふくもすずしく
なりたいもんね・・・。

あちー・・・

Boy: はやく衣がえに
ならないかな・・・。
I hope we get to switch
our uniforms soon...

あちー・・・ ("It's so hot...")

Girl: ふだんの衣るいだけじゃなくて
せいふくもすずしくなりたいもんね・・・。
Even if you're wearing summer clothes
at home, we still have to wear these hot
uniforms at school a little longer...

(Japanese schools have a specific day on which students can stop wearing their winter uniforms and begin wearing their summer ones ... but sometimes the hot weather arrives before that day!)

坂

SLOPE / HILL

さか、ハン

ex. 坂 (さか) - hill
ex. 坂道 (さかみち) - hillside road
ex. 上り坂 (のぼりざか) - ascent

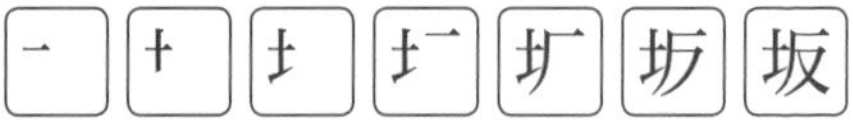

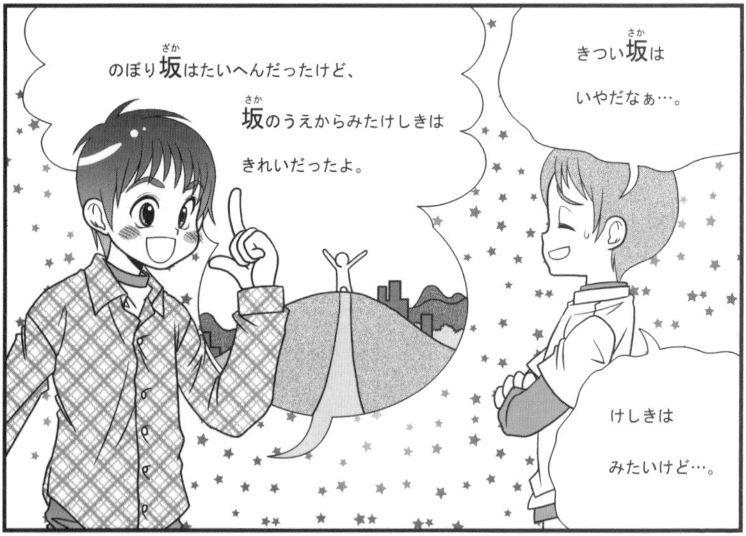
のぼり坂はたいへんだったけど、
坂のうえからみたけしきは
きれいだったよ。
きつい坂は
いやだなぁ…。
けしきは
みたいけど…。

First boy: のぼり坂はたいへんだったけど、坂のうえからみたけしきはきれいだったよ。
It was rough climbing up that hill, but there was a nice view from the top.

Second boy: きつい坂はいやだなぁ・・・。
Steep hills are no fun...
けしきはみたいけど・・・。
...though I wouldn't mind seeing the view from the top.

FLOURISH / GLORY

さか(える)、は(える)、エイ

ex. 栄養* (えいよう) - nutrition
ex. 栄える (さかえる) - to flourish
ex. 繁栄* (はんえい) - thriving

丶	丷	⺍	𭕄	𰀁	𰀂	学
栄	栄					

栄

きょうりゅうはちゅうせいだいにはん栄したいきものだね。
りゅうはわからないけど・・・。
でもそんなに栄えていたのに、なぜほろんじゃったのかしら？
いま栄えていたらたいへんだね・・・。
そうね・・・。
恐竜

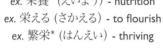

Boy: きょうりゅうはちゅうせいだいにはん栄したいきものだね。Dinosaurs thrived during the Mesozoic era.
Girl: でもそんなに栄えていたのに、なぜほろんじゃったのかしら？ If they were flourishing, why did they become extinct?
Boy: りゅうはわからないけど・・・。I don't know the reason, but... いま栄えていたらたいへんだね・・・。If they were thriving now, life would be pretty tough for us...
Girl: そうね・・・。It sure would...
Book title: 恐竜 (Dinosaurs)

DECIDE

さだ(まる)、さだ(める)、ジョウ、テイ

ex. 案の定 (あんのじょう) - as expected
ex. 定める (さだめる) - to decide
ex. 断定* (だんてい) - conclusion

| ' | '' | 宀 | 宀 | 宇 | 宇 | 宇 |

| 定 | | | | | | |

べんきょうさぼって
ねているわね。

そんなだん定
しなくても…。

あんの定
ねているわね。

おしおきー！！

そんなこと
定めてないだろ！！

Big sister: べんきょうさぼって
ねているわね。
He's in there sleeping instead
of studying, isn't he?

Little sister: そんなだん定
しなくても･･･。How did you
come to that conclusion...

ぐうぐう (snoring)
Big sister: あんの定ねているわね。
Just as I thought, he's asleep.
おしおきー！！ You need to be punished!!
ぐりぐり (thump-thump on head)
Brother: そんなこと定めてないだろ！！
You aren't the one who decides that!!

MANNER

さま、ヨウ

ex. 様々 (さまざま) - varied
ex. 仏様 (ほとけさま) - Buddha
ex. 様子 (ようす) - state

様

げきはどんな様(よう)す？
ひょこっ
いいんじゃないかしら。
ほっ
みんなじぶんのやくが
様(さま)になっているし。

Director: げきはどんな様す？
How is the play shaping up?

ひょこっ (peeking out)

Stage manager: いいんじゃないかしら。
Not half bad, I'd say.

Stage manager: みんなじぶんのやくが様になっているし。
Everyone is getting into their character and all.

ほっ (sigh of relief)

ROUTE

じ、ロ

ex. 家路 (いえじ) - the road home
ex. 順路* (じゅんろ) - route
ex. 路地 (ろじ) - lane

路

| 丨 | 冂 | 口 | 吊 | 吊 | 趴 | 毘 |
| 趴 | 趴 | 趺 | 趽 | 路 | 路 | |

ゆうひをせにして
いえ路につきました。
おしまい・・・っと。

このはなし
おもしろかったなぁ。

よみながらあるいていたら
路じに
まよいこんじゃった
みたい・・・。

ここどこだろう。

Boy (reading): ゆうひをせにしていえ路につきました。おしまい・・・っと。
"With his back to the setting sun, he arrived on the road leading home. The end."
このはなしおもしろかったなぁ。
That was a pretty good story.

はっ ("Huh?")
よみながらあるいていたら路じにまよいこんじゃったみたい・・・。
ここどこだろう。
It looks like I lost my way while reading and walking at the same time...
Where am I?

SALT

しお、エン

ex. 塩水 (えんすい) - salt water
ex. 塩素* (えんそ) - chlorine
ex. 塩分 (えんぶん) - sodium

しょっぱい！！

塩(しお)いれすぎ

ちゃったみたい・・・。

塩(えん)ぶんのとりすぎは

けんこうにもわるいし。

きをつけ

なくちゃ・・・。

Chef in training: しょっぱい！！
Salty!!

塩いれすぎちゃったみたい・・・。
It looks like I put in too much salt...

Bottle label: 塩 (salt)

塩分のとりすぎはけんこうにもわるいし。
Too much sodium is bad for your health too.

きをつけなくちゃ・・・。I should be more careful.

島

ISLAND

しま、トウ

ex. 島流し (しまながし) - exile
ex. 無人島* (むじんとう) - desert island
ex. 離島* (りとう) - faraway island

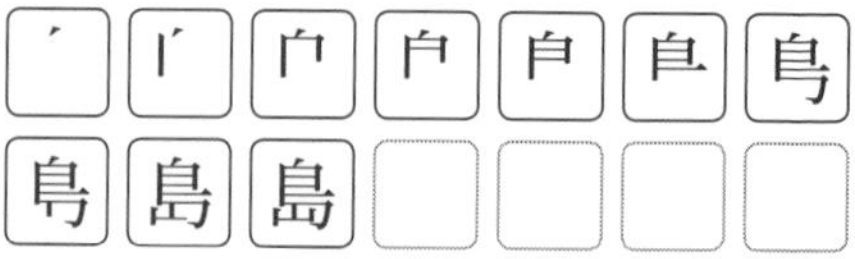

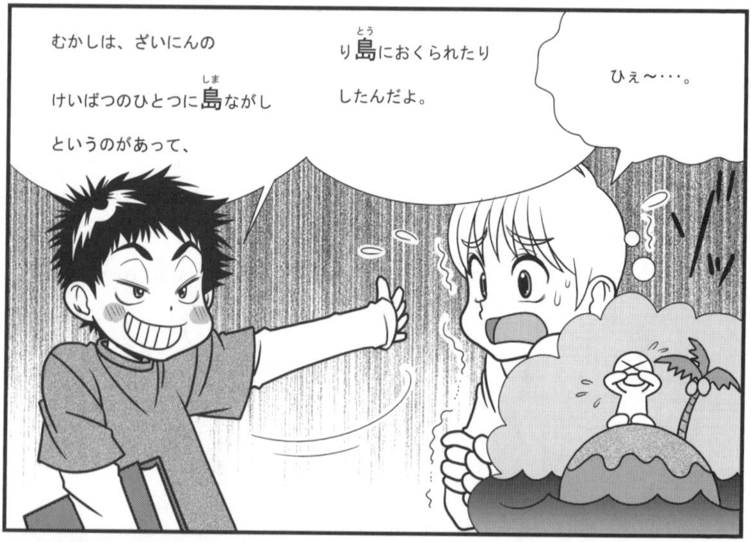
むかしは、ざいにんの
けいばつのひとつに島(しま)ながし
というのがあって、
り島(とう)におくられたり
したんだよ。
ひぇ〜・・・。
ゾッ

Fist boy: むかしは、ざいにんのけいばつのひとつに島ながしというのがあって、り島におくられたりしたんだよ。
A long time ago, people were sent into exile as a form of punishment. They would be banished to faraway islands.

Second boy: ひぇ〜・・・。
Eeek...

ゾッ (quivering with fear)

INVESTIGATE

調

しら(べる)、チョウ

ex. 調べる(しらべる) - to examine
ex. 順調* (じゅんちょう) - favorable
ex. 調子 (ちょうし) - condition

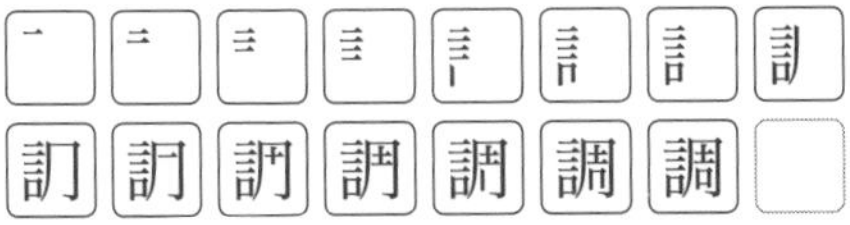

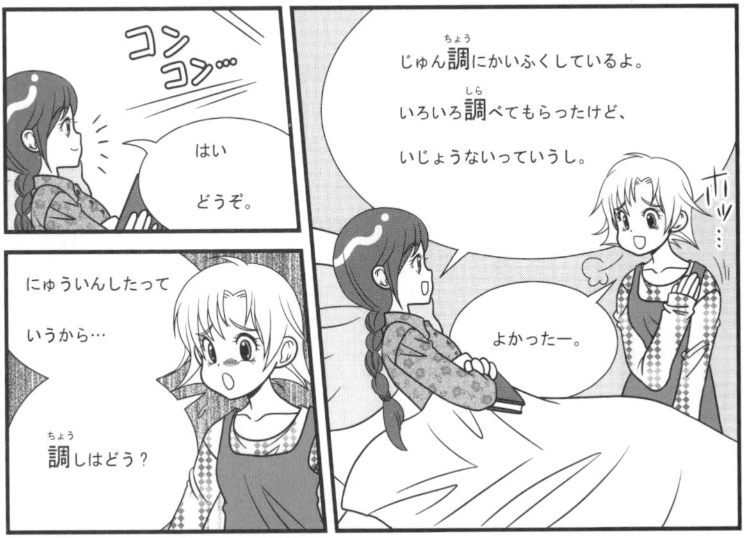
コンコン…
はい どうぞ。
にゅういんしたって いうから…
調しはどう？
じゅん調にかいふくしているよ。 いろいろ調べてもらったけど、 いじょうないっていうし。
ホッ…
よかったー。

コンコン・・・ (knock-knock)
First girl: はいどうぞ。
Yes, come in.
Second girl: にゅういんしたっていうから・・・ 調しはどう？
I heard you were in the hospital... How do you feel?
First girl: じゅん調にかいふくしているよ。いろいろ調べてもらったけど、いじょうないっていうし。I'm doing just fine. The doctors gave me a thorough examination, and they said there's nothing abnormal.
Second girl: よかったー。That's great news.
ホッ・・・ (sigh of relief)

STAMP / SEAL

しるし、じるし、イン

ex. 印鑑* (いんかん) - stamp
ex. 印象* (いんしょう) - impression
ex. 目印 (めじるし) - mark

ˊ 厂 F E 臼 印

ヤマダさんの
にもつってどれ？

はこのそくめんに
印かんがおして
あるやつよ。

たしかにこれは
めだつ印だ…。

Boy: ヤマダさんのにもつってどれ？
Which package is for Mr. Yamada?

Girl: はこのそくめんに印かんがおして
あるやつよ。
It's the one with the big stamp on the
side.

Boy: たしかにこれはめだつ印だ・・・。
That stamp definitely does stand out...

Stamp on box: 山田 (Yamada; the 田 is
not visible in this illustration.)

CONNECTION

せき、カン

ex. 関心 (かんしん) - concern; interest
ex. 玄関 (げんかん) - vestibule
ex. 関所 (せきしょ) - checkpoint

関

ドロドロ
ただい・・・
ま・・・!?
!
げん関（かん）からいえにはいるまえに、
にわのすいどうでそのドロをおとしてきなさい！
はーい・・・。
まるで
関（せき）しょ・・・。

ドロドロ
(covered in mud)

Boy: ただい・・・
ま・・・！？
I'm ho... home!?

Mother: げん関からいえにはいるまえに、
にわのすいどうでそのドロをおとしてきなさい！
Before you set foot out of the doorway and into my house, you go back to the yard and hose yourself down right now!

Boy: はーい・・・。 まるで関しょ・・・。
OK already... It's like a checkpoint...

反

OPPOSE/COUNTER

そ(らす)、そ(る)、ハン、ホン、タン

ex. 反らす (そらす) - to warp; to bend
ex. 反対 (はんたい) - opposition
ex. 反応* (はんのう) - reaction

一	厂	万	反			

むりしないほうがいいよ…。
どんなに反(はん)たいされようとも、
どのくらいからだを反(そ)らせられるか、やってみたかったんだ・・・。
……。
ぷる
ぷる
ぷる
ぷる・・・

Sister: むりしないほうがいいよ・・・。
I don't think you should push yourself...

Brother: どんなに反たいされようとも、
No matter how much you object...

Brother: どのくらいからだを反らせられるか、やってみたかったんだ・・・。
...I'm going to find out how far back I can bend.

Sister: (speechless)

ぷるぷる・・・ (muscles twitching)

EVEN

たい(ら)、ひら、ヘイ、ビョウ

ex. 平ら (たいら) - flat; level
ex. 手の平 (てのひら) - palm
ex. 平常心* (へいじょうしん) - one's cool

一	二	丁	平	平			

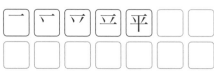

あ！ヤマダくんだ。

平じょうしん・・・
平じょうしん・・・。

ニヤニヤ

たいへんだ！！
ての平もかおも
まっかだよ！！

どこか平らなところで
やすんだほうが
いいよ。

Lovestruck girl: あ！
ヤマダくんだ。
平じょうしん・・・
平じょうしん・・・
Oh! It's Yamada-kun. Stay
cool... stay cool...
ニヤニヤ (snickering)

Yamada: たいへんだ！！ての平もかおもまっかだよ！！
Oh, no!! Her palms and face are all red!!

か〜・・・ (blushing)

どこか平らなところでやすんだほうがいいよ。
We've got to get you someplace where you can
lay down and rest.

帳

NOTEBOOK

チョウ

ex. 几帳面* (きちょうめん) - punctual

ex. 通帳 (つうちょう) - bankbook

ex. 手帳 (てちょう) - day planner

らいねんようのて帳(ちょう)・・・
だって、りょうほうともかわいいんだもん。
どっちにしようかまよっちゃう・・・。

Girl: らいねんようのて帳・・・
My day planner for next year...

どっちにしようかまよっちゃう・・・。
I can't decide which one to choose...

だって、りょうほうともかわいいんだもん。
They're just both so cute.

CITY BLOCK

チョウ、テイ

ex. 丁寧* (ていねい) - careful; proper
ex. 一丁 (いっちょう) - one serving (of food)
ex. 丁目 (ちょうめ) - block number

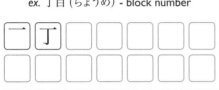

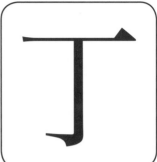

ごちゅう
もんは？

カツどんひとつ。

てい
丁ねいなちずのおかげで
すんなりもくてきの
しょくどうについちゃった。

カツどん
いっ丁!!

Man: 丁ねいなちずのおかげで
すんなりもくてきのしょくどうに
ついちゃった。Thanks to that
carefully written map, I was able to
find this restaurant pretty easily.

カラカラカラ (sliding door)

Waiter: ごちゅうもんは？
Can I take your order?
Man: カツどんひとつ。
One katsudon, please.
Waiter: カツどんいっ丁!!
One order of katsudon!!
(Katsudon is a fried pork cutlet served over rice in a bowl.)

鉄

IRON

テツ

ex. 鉄アレイ (てつアレイ) - iron dumbbell
ex. 鉄道 (てつどう) - railroad
ex. 鉄板 (てっぱん) - iron skillet

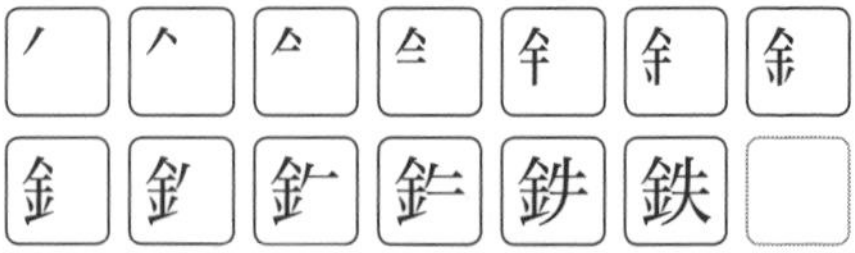

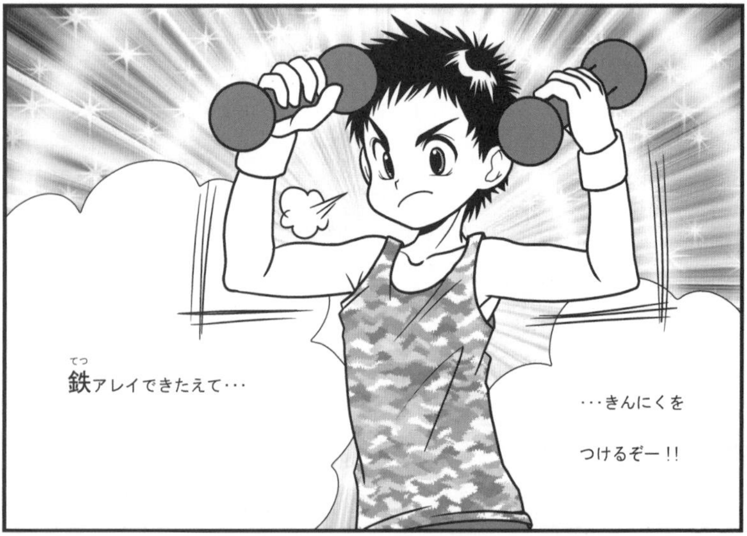

鉄(てつ)アレイできたえて･･･
･･･きんにくを
つけるぞー!!

Athlete: 鉄アレイできたえて ･･･
I'm gonna train with these iron dumbbells...

･･･ きんにくをつけるぞー!!
...and then I'll have some real muscles!!

FLOW

流

なが(す)、なが(れる)、リュウ 、ル

ex. 流れる (ながれる) - to flow
ex. 風流 (ふうりゅう) - elegance
ex. 流行 (りゅうこう) - fashionable

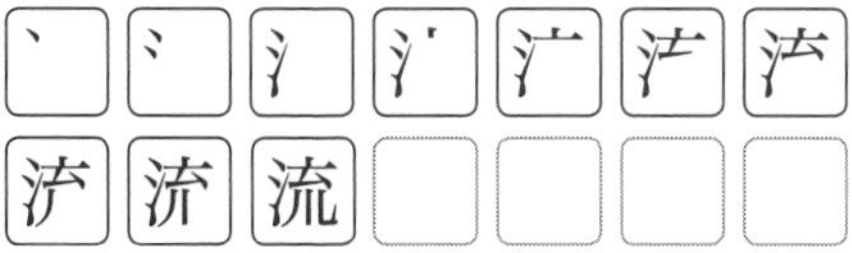

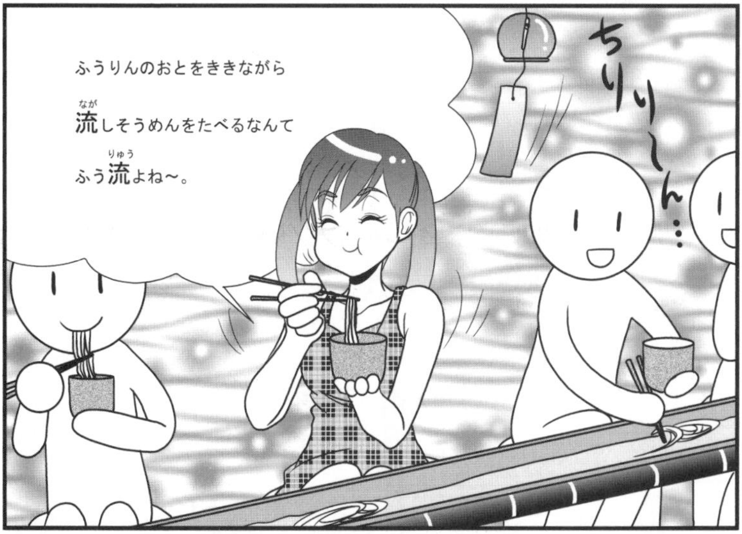
ふうりんのおとをききながら
なが
流しそうめんをたべるなんて
りゅう
ふう流よね〜。
ちりり〜ん・・・

Girl: ふうりんのおとをききながら流しそうめんをたべるなんてふう流よね〜。
Listening to the sound of a wind chime while eating nagashi somen makes me feel so elegant and refined.

ちりり〜ん・・・ (ringing of wind chime)

(Nagashi somen is a traditional Japanese way of eating cold noodles out of a bamboo water chute. It's typically enjoyed during summer festivals.)

THROW

な(げる)、トウ

ex. 投函* (とうかん) - mail
ex. 投票* (とうひょう) - vote
ex. 投げる (なげる) - to throw

一 亅 扌 扩 扣 投 投

でかけるの？

うん。てがみを
投かんしてくる。

じゃぁ、これもついでに
投かんしてきて。

投げないで
ちゃんとわたしてよ。

Younger sister: でかけるの？
Are you going out?

Older sister: うん。てがみを
投かんしてくる。
Yeah, I'm going to go mail a letter.

Younger sister: じゃぁ、これもついでに
投かんしてきて。Well, mail this one too.

ぽいっ (toss)

Older sister: 投げないで
ちゃんとわたしてよ。
Don't throw it, hand it to me.

WAVE

なみ、ハ

ex. 津波* (つなみ) - tsunami
ex. 電波 (でんぱ) - radio waves; reception
ex. 波浪警報* (はろうけいほう) - wave alert

` ｀ ｀ ｀ ｀ ｀ 波 波

たいふうのせいりょくは

ましてきており、

このかいがんふきん

には波ろうけいほう

がだされています！！

うわー！！

すごい波！！！

Reporter: たいふうのせいりょくはましてきており、このかいがんふきんには波ろうけいほうがだされています！！ The typhoon continues to grow stronger, so we'll be broadcasting wave alerts for the coastal regions!!

ザッパーン・・ (waves crashing)

Viewers: うわー！！！すごい波！！！ Whoa!! Those are some amazing waves!!!

庭

YARD

にわ、テイ

ex. 裏庭* (うらにわ) - backyard
ex. 家庭 (かてい) - household
ex. 校庭 (こうてい) - campus

すごい庭(にわ)ですねー！
まるで庭(てい)えんみたいですね。
いや～・・・
それほどでも。

First boy: すごい庭ですねー！
まるで庭えんみたいですね。
What an amazing backyard!
It's almost like a park.

Second Boy: いや～・・・
それほどでも。
You know...
I think it's even better.

PRACTICE

練

ね(る)、レン

ex. 訓練* (くんれん) - practice; training
ex. 洗練* (せんれん) - refinement
ex. 練る (ねる) - to work over

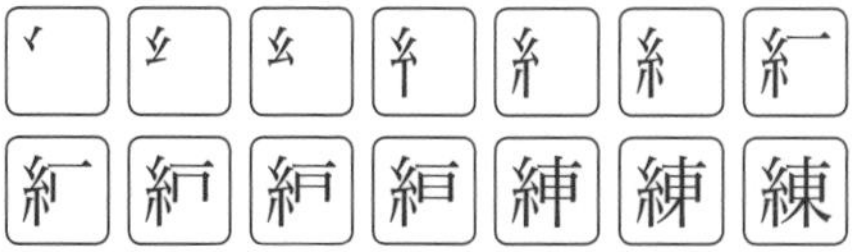

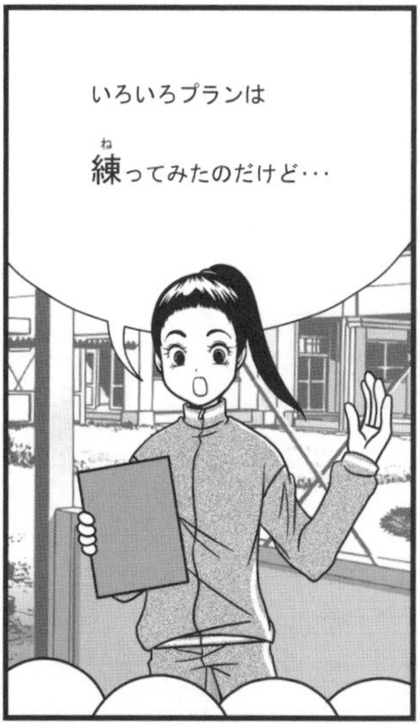
いろいろプランは練ってみたのだけど・・・

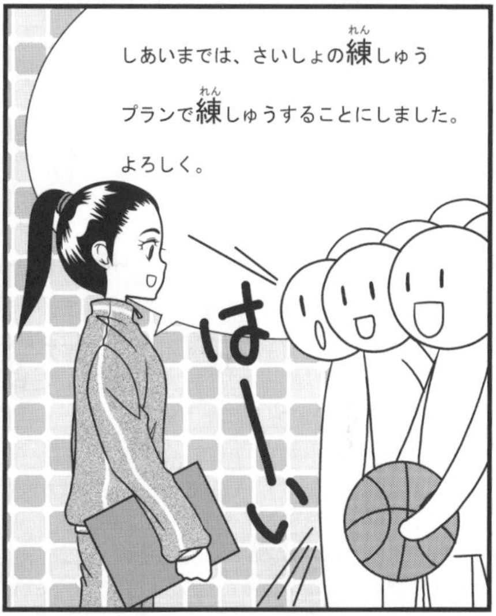
しあいまでは、さいしょの練しゅうプランで練しゅうすることにしました。よろしく。
はーい

Coach: いろいろプランは練ってみたのだけど・・・
I know we've worked over quite a few different plans...

しあいまでは、さいしょの練しゅうプランで練しゅうすることにしました。よろしく。
But until the next match, I think we should stick to our original practice plan. I'm counting on you.

Teammates (in unison): はーい OK!

農

AGRICULTURE

ノウ

ex. 農家 (のうか) - farm family
ex. 農業 (のうぎょう) - agriculture
ex. 酪農* (らくのう) - dairy farm

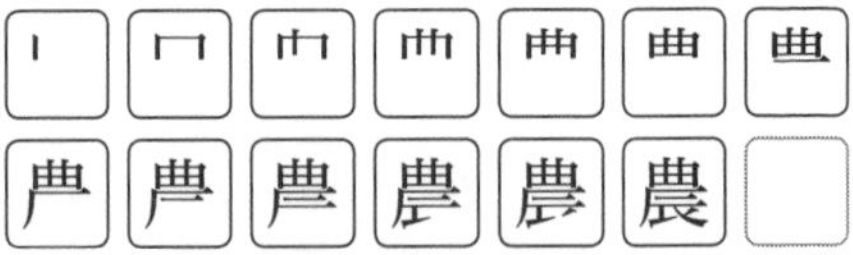

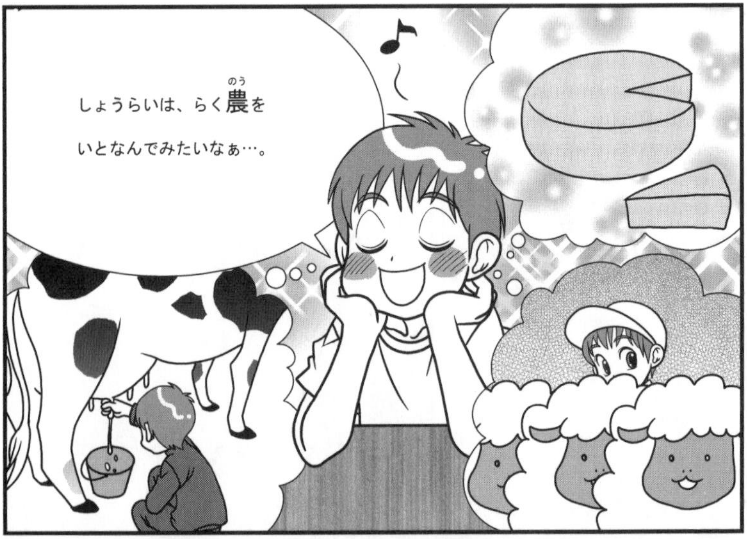
しょうらいは、らく農をいとなんでみたいなぁ…。

Boy: しょうらいは、らく農を
いとなんでみたいなぁ・・・。
I'd love to run a dairy farm when I grow up...

CLIMB

のぼ（る）、ト、トウ、

ex. 登場 (とうじょう) - come out; appear
ex. 登録* (とうろく) - register
ex. 登る (のぼる) - to climb

フ｜ダ｜ダ´｜癶｜癶｜癶｜癶
癶｜癶｜癶｜癶｜登

しゅじんこうは、この
はしごを登って…

ここから登じょうすること。
わかった？

はーい。

Stagehand: しゅじんこうは、この
はしごを登って・・・
So the main actor will climb
up this ladder...

ここから登じょうすること。わかった？
And come out from here. Understood?

Actors (in unison): はーい。
Yes!

葉

LEAF

は、ヨウ

ex. 葉っぱ (はっぱ) - leaf

ex. 葉巻* (はまき) - cigar

ex. 葉脈* (ようみゃく) - veins of a leaf

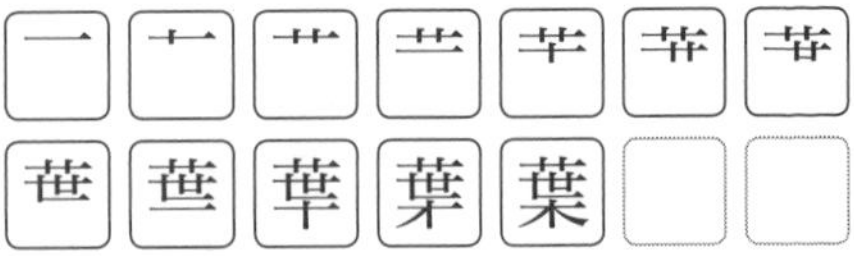

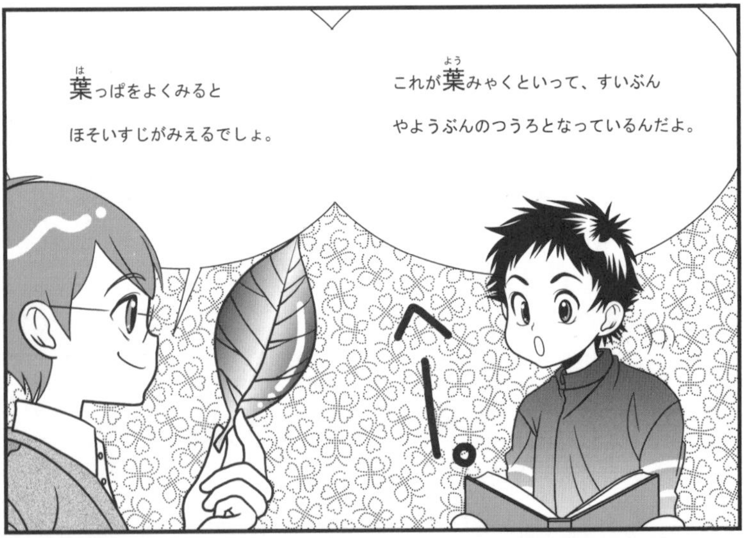
葉っぱをよくみると
ほそいすじがみえるでしょ。
これが葉みゃくといって、すいぶん
やようぶんのつうろとなっているんだよ。
へー。

Teacher: 葉っぱをよくみると ほそいすじがみえるでしょ。 If you look carefully at a leaf you can see a bunch of lines, right?

これが葉みゃくといって、すいぶんやようぶんのつうろとなっているんだよ。 These are called the veins of the leaf, they act as a passageway for the plant's moisture and nutrition.

Student: へー。Wow...

TIMES/DOUBLE

バイ

ex. 倍数（ばいすう）- multiple
ex. 倍率*（ばいりつ）- scale; factor
ex. 人一倍（ひといちばい）- unusual

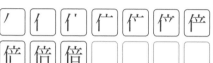

倍

ノ 亻 亻' 亻亠 亻亠丷 亻立 亻立
倍 倍 倍

うけたいがっこうの倍(ばい)りつ
すごくたかいなぁ…。
はぁ…
よーし！いまよりなん倍(ばい)もべんきょうして
ぜったいごうかくするぞー!!

Student: うけたいがっこうの倍りつすごくたかいなぁ・・・
The grading scale of the school I want to get into sure is high...

はぁ・・・ (sigh)

よーし！いまよりなん倍もべんきょうしてぜったいごうかくするぞー！！
All right! I'll just study a million times harder so I get in for sure!!

箱

BOX

はこ

ex. 私書箱 (ししょばこ) - P.O. box
ex. びっくり箱 (びっくりばこ) - jack-in-the-box
ex. 筆箱 (ふでばこ) - pencil case

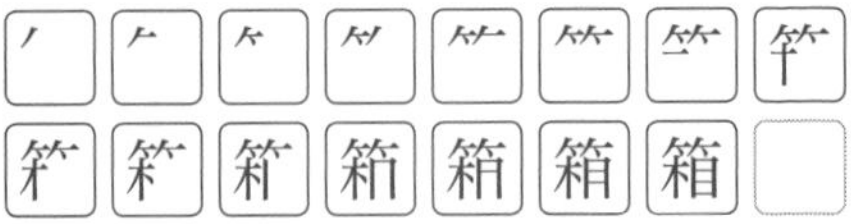

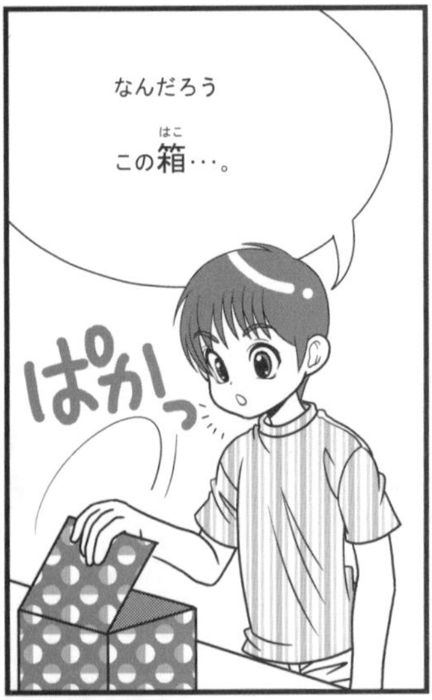
なんだろう
この箱(はこ)・・・。
ぱかっ

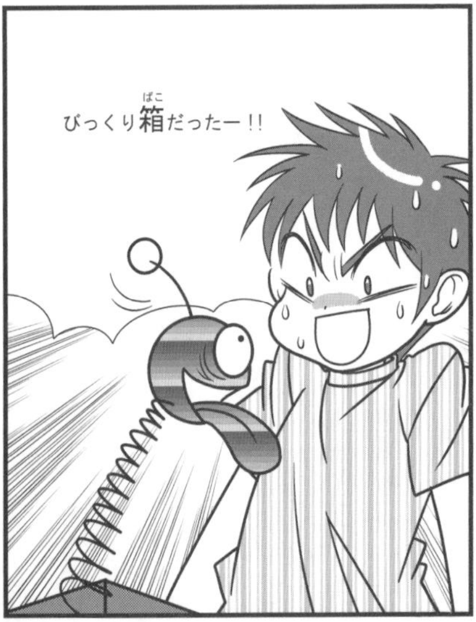
びっくり箱(ばこ)だったー!!

Boy: なんだろうこの箱・・・。
I wonder what this box is for...

ぱかっ (lid being lifted)

びっくり箱だったー!!
It's a jack-in-the-box!!

PILLAR

柱

はしら、チュウ

ex. 霜柱* (しもばしら) - icicle
ex. 電柱 (でんちゅう) - telephone pole
ex. 柱時計 (はしらどけい) - grandfather clock

一	十	才	木	木`	木亠	杧
柱	柱					

ねぇ…
この柱(はしら)ぐらぐらしてない？
ぐらぐら
ほんとうだ！
ぐらぐら
ぐらぐら
柱(はしら)をほきょうしないと このたてもの こわれちゃうよ !!

Big sister: ねぇ・・・
この柱ぐらぐらしてない？
Hey... Doesn't this pillar seem kinda wobbly?

ぐらぐら (wobble-wobble)

Little brother: ほんとうだ！ You're right!

Little brother: 柱をほきょうしないと
このたてものこわれちゃうよ！！
If we don't reinforce these pillars, this treehouse is gonna fall apart!!

畑

FIELD

はた、はたけ

ex. 畑違い* (はたけちがい) - outside one's field

ex. 畑作 (はたさく) - dry-field farming

ex. 花畑 (はなばたけ) - flower bed

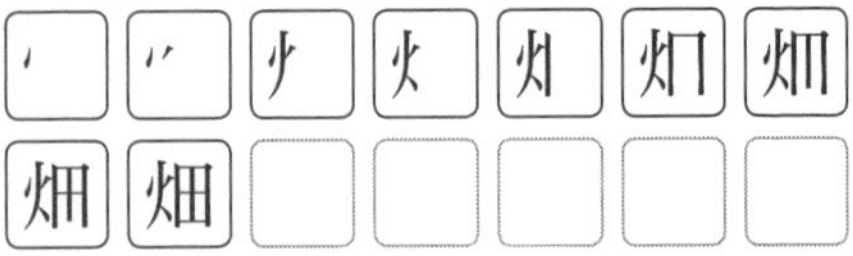

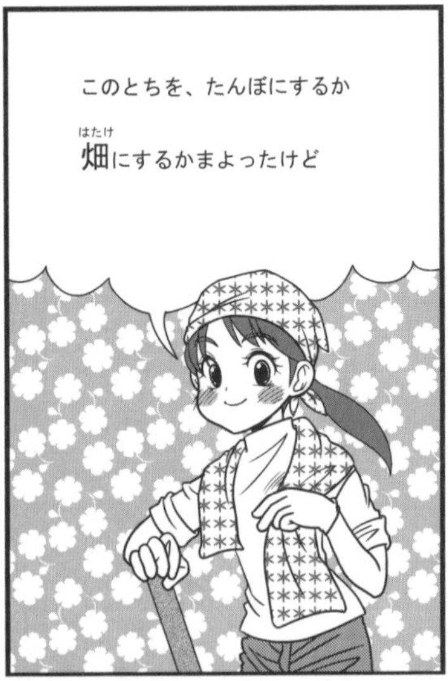
このとちを、たんぼにするか
畑にするかまよったけど

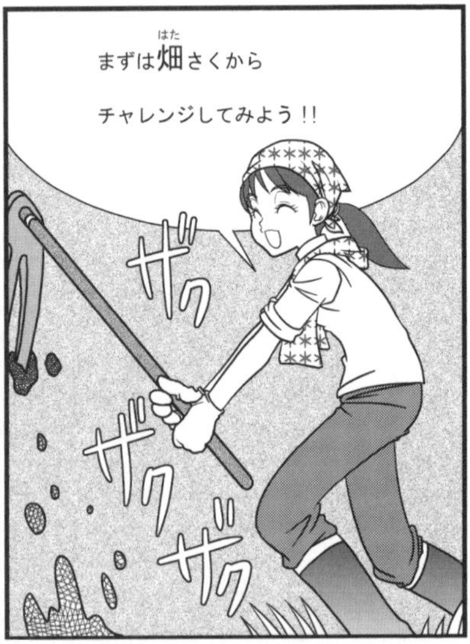
まずは畑さくから
チャレンジしてみよう!!
ザク
ザク
ザク

Farmer: このとちを、たんぼにするか
畑にするかまよったけど
I'm not sure if I should use this land for a fruit field or rice field, but...

まずは畑さくから
チャレンジしてみよう!!
I'll start by taking on the dry field first!!

ザクザクザク (tilling soil)

FRUIT

は(たす)、は(てる)、カ

ex. 果汁* (かじゅう) - fruit juice
ex. 果物 (くだもの) - fruit
ex. 果たす (はたす) - to carry out

| 丨 | 冂 | 円 | 日 | 旦 | 甲 | 果 |
| 果 | | | | | | |

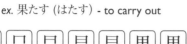

よし、これで果<ruby>物<rt>くだ</rt></ruby>を
ぜんぶしゅうかくできたぞ。

しゅうかくする

せきにんは

<ruby>果<rt>は</rt></ruby>たせたな。

おつかれさま。<ruby>果<rt>か</rt></ruby>じゅう１００％の

ジュースでものんでやすんでね。

おいしい！！

Farmer: よし、これで果ものをぜんぶしゅうかくできたぞ。 All right, with this I'll have gathered all of the fruit.
しゅうかくするせきにんは果たせたな。 Now I'm done with the harvest.
ふう・・・ (exhale)　ドサ・・・ (placing a heavy object)

Wife: おつかれさま。果じゅう１００％のジュースでものんでやすんでね。 Great job. Why don't you take a break and enjoy some 100% fruit juice?

Farmer: おいしい！！ Delicious!!

RELEASE

放

はな(す)、はな(つ)、はな(れる)、ホウ

ex. 食べ放題 (たべほうだい) - all-you-can-eat
ex. 放す (はなす) - to let go
ex. 放置* (ほうち) - to neglect

あそこで
ふうせん
くばってるよ。

そう？

あ！
放しちゃった・・・

またくれると

いいけど・・・

・・・・・・。

あそこは
たべ放だいでしょう。

うん！！

First boy: あそこでふうせんくばってるよ。Hey,
they're giving away balloons over there.
ふわふわ (floating lightly)
Second boy: そう？Really? あそこはたべ放だい
でしょう。That's the all you can eat place.
First boy: うん！！Yeah!!
ぱっ (letting go)　ふわり・・・ (drifting away)

First boy: あ！はなしちゃった・・・
Oops! I let it go...
ふわ・・・ (floating lightly)
またくれるといいけど・・・
I hope I can get another...

Second boy: (speechless)

SHEEP

ひつじ、ヨウ

ex. 子羊 (こひつじ) - lamb
ex. 牧羊犬* (ぼくようけん) - sheepdog
ex. 羊毛 (ようもう) - wool

羊^{よう}もうって

なんだろう？

羊^{ひつじ}ややぎなどの

けのことよ。

うわー、

あたたかそう。

Boy: 羊もうってなんだろう？
What is "wool" anyway?

Girl: 羊ややぎなどのけのことよ。
It means that it's made from the hair of animals like sheep and goats.

Boy: うわー、あたたかそう。
Wow, sounds nice and warm.

等

EQUAL

ひと(しい)、トウ

ex. 等 (とう) - etc.
ex. 等身大 (とうしんだい) - life-size
ex. 等分 (とうぶん) - equal parts

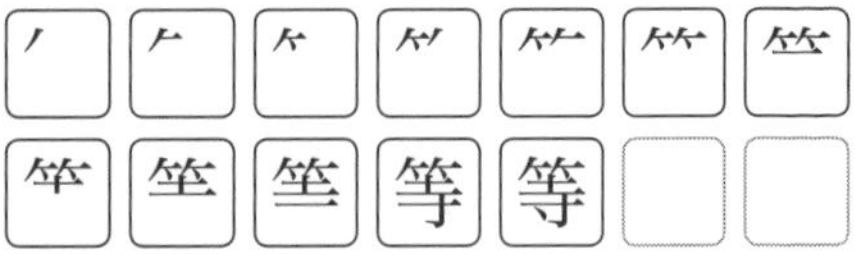

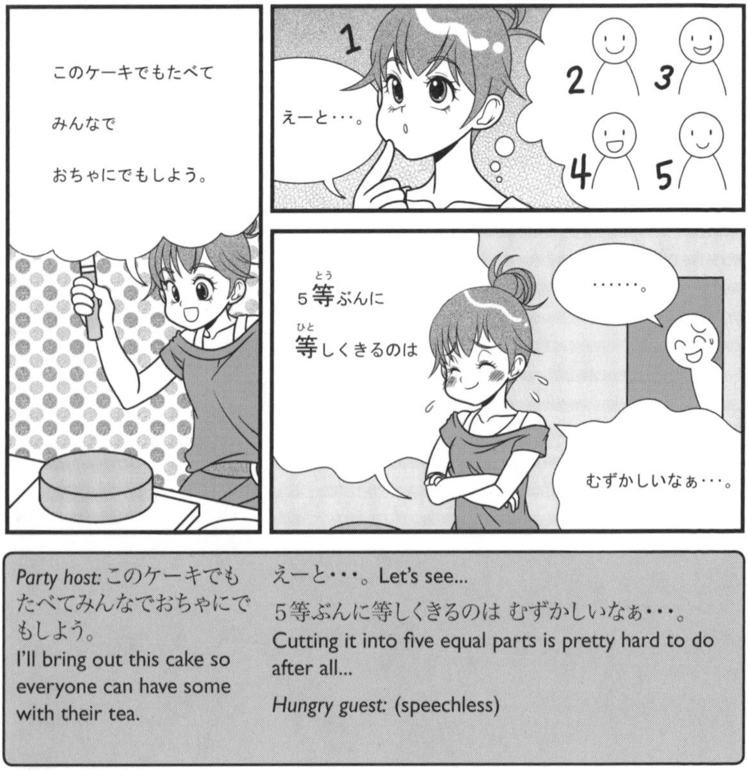
このケーキでもたべて
みんなで
おちゃにでもしよう。
1
えーと・・・。
2
3
4
5
5 等(とう)ぶんに
等(ひと)しくきるのは
……。
むずかしいなぁ・・・。

Party host: このケーキでもたべてみんなでおちゃにでもしよう。
I'll bring out this cake so everyone can have some with their tea.

えーと・・・。 Let's see...

5等ぶんに等しくきるのは むずかしいなぁ・・・。
Cutting it into five equal parts is pretty hard to do after all...

Hungry guest: (speechless)

SECTION

ブ

ex. 部長（ぶちょう）- chief; department head
ex. 部品（ぶひん）- parts
ex. 部分（ぶぶん）- portion

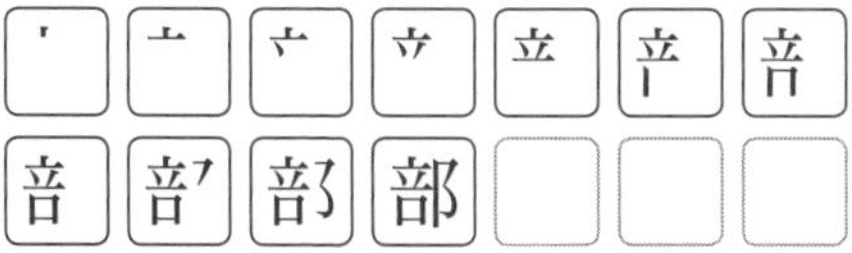

`	立	立	立	立	辛	音
音	音	部	部			

ラジコンぜん**部**かんせい！！

あとは

はしらせるだけ・・・。

ポロ…

・・・・・・。

どの**部**ぶんにつかう

ねじなんだろう…。

この**部**ひんのために

ぶんかいするのはいやだなぁ。

Boy: ラジコンぜん部かんせい！！
My radio-controlled car is completely finished!!

あとははしらせるだけ・・・。
All that's left is to make it go...
ポロ・・・ (screw falling out)

(Speechless)

どの部ぶんにつかうねじなんだろう・・・。
What part could that screw have been for?

この部ひんのためにぶんかいする

のはいやだなぁ。I don't want to take the whole thing apart just for this one piece.

FLUTE / WHISTLE

ふえ、テキ

ex. 口笛（くちぶえ）- whistling
ex. 鼓笛隊*（こてきたい）- marching band
ex. 縦笛*（たてぶえ）- recorder

ねっしんに**笛**の
れんしゅうをしているんだね。

こ**笛**たいの
笛のれんしゅうなんだ。

がんばってね。

First boy: ねっしんに笛のれんしゅう
をしているんだね。
You've really been practicing that
recorder like crazy lately.

Second boy: こ笛たいの笛のれんしゅうな
んだ。
I'm practicing the recorder for the
marching band.

First boy: がんばってね。
Well, do your best!

FORTUNE

福

フク

ex. 福音 (ふくいん) - good news; gospel
ex. 福祉* (ふくし) - social security
ex. 裕福* (ゆうふく) - prosperity

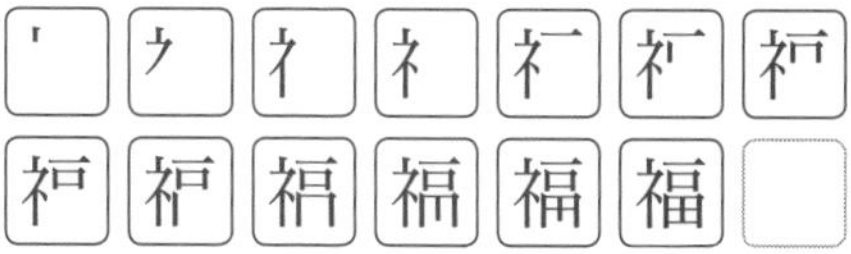

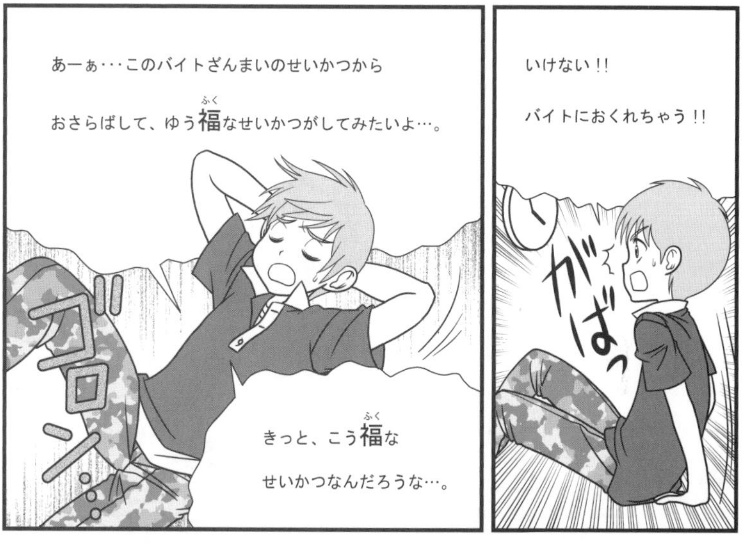
あーぁ・・・このバイトざんまいのせいかつから
おさらばして、ゆう福なせいかつがしてみたいよ…。
ゴロン・・・
きっと、こう福な
せいかつなんだろうな…。
いけない!!
バイトにおくれちゃう!!
がばっ

Boy: あーぁ・・・このバイトざんまいのせいかつからおさらばして、ゆう福なせいかつがしてみたいよ・・・。
Ahh... I'd like to say goodbye to all my part-time jobs and enjoy a life of wealth and luxury...
きっと、こう福なせいかつなんだろうな・・・。
It's got to be the epitome of happiness...
ゴロン・・・ (rolling around in bed)

いけない!!バイトにおくれちゃう!!
Oh no!! I'm gonna be late for my part-time job!!
がばっ
(getting up suddenly)

LOSE

ま(かす)、ま(ける)、お(う)、フ

ex. 勝負 (しょうぶ) - a match
ex. 負傷* (ふしょう) - injury
ex. 負ける (まける) - to lose

ノ　ク　イ　名　角　角　負

負　負

きのうあしを負しょう

しなければ

きょうのしあい

負けなかったのにな・・・。

Soccer player: きのうあしを負しょうしなければ
きょうのしあい負けなかったのにな・・・。
If only I hadn't injured my foot yesterday,
we wouldn't have lost today's game...

BOULEVARD

まち、カイ、ガイ

ex. 街路樹* (がいろじゅ) - roadside trees
ex. 商店街 (しょうてんがい) - shopping arcade
ex. 街並 (まちなみ) - townscape

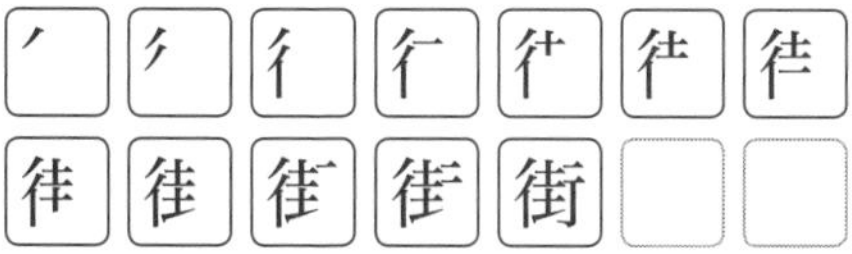

街

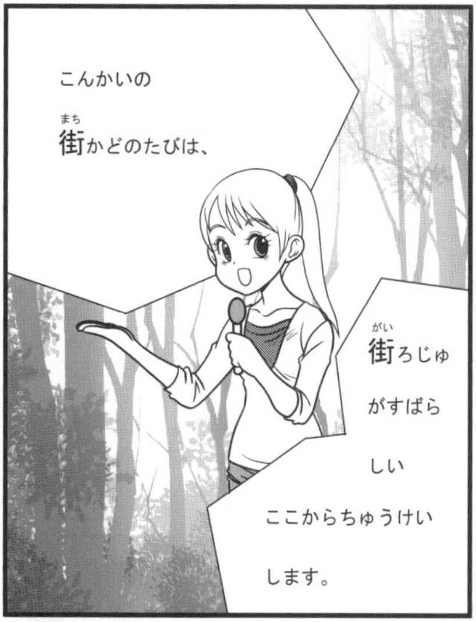
こんかいの
まち
街かどのたびは、
がい
街ろじゅ
がすばら
しい
ここからちゅうけい
します。

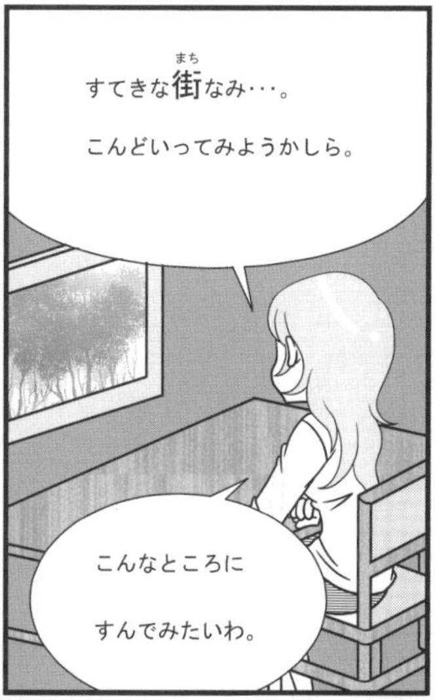
まち
すてきな街なみ・・・。
こんどいってみようかしら。
こんなところに
すんでみたいわ。

Reporter: こんかいの街かどのたびは、
This time on "Street Corner Traveller..."
街ろじゅがすばらしいここからちゅうけいします。
...we're broadcasting from this boulevard flanked by magnificent trees.

Viewer: すてきな街なみ・・・。こんどいってみようかしら。
What a charming area... Maybe I should check it out some time.
こんなところにすんでみたいわ。
I'd love to live in a place like that.

豆

BEAN

まめ、ズ、トウ、

ex. 大豆 (だいず) - soybeans
ex. 豆腐* (とうふ) - tofu
ex. 納豆* (なっとう) - fermented soybeans

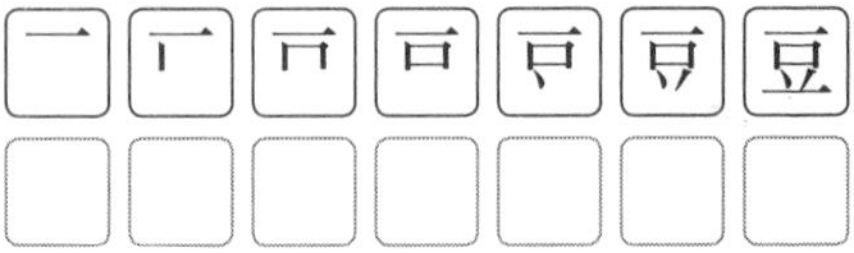

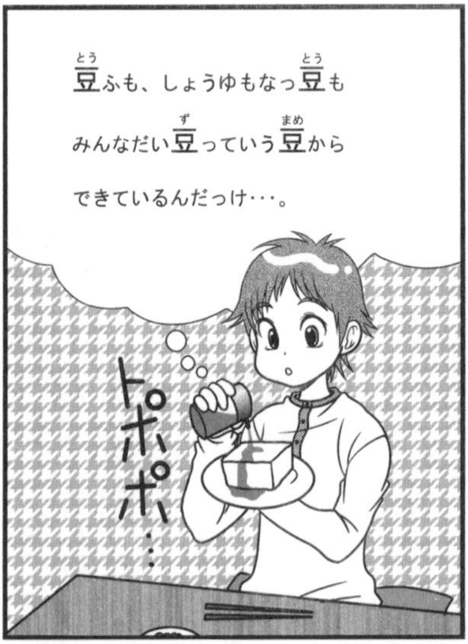
豆ふも、しょうゆもなっ豆も
みんなだい豆っていう豆から
できているんだっけ・・・。
トポポ・・・

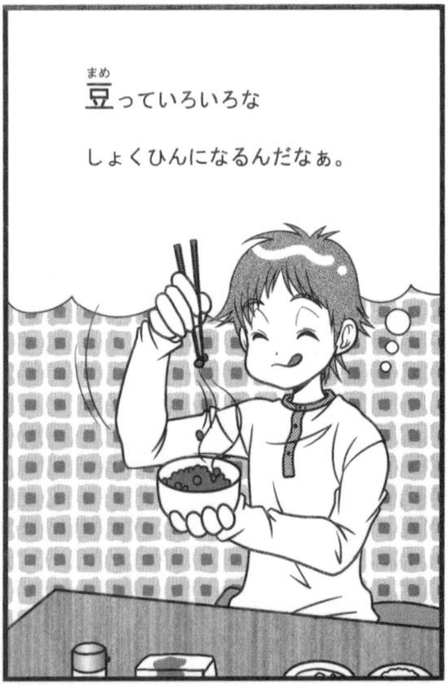
豆っていろいろな
しょくひんになるんだなぁ。

Girl: 豆ふも、しょうゆもなっ豆もみんなだい豆っていう豆からできているんだっけ・・・。
Tofu, soy sauce and fermented soybeans are all made from soybeans aren't they ...
トポポ・・・ (sauce being poured)

豆っていろいろなしょくひんになるんだなぁ。
There sure are a lot of different foods that can be made out of beans.

GREEN

みどり、リョク、ロク

ex. 緑茶 (りょくちゃ) - green tea
ex. 緑化 (りょっか) - tree-planting
ex. 緑色 (みどりいろ) - green-colored

おおぜいでなにを
しているの？

あぁ、
これはね。

緑(りょく)かうんどうで、緑(みどり)をふやそうと
こうえんでごみひろいや
かだんのていれを
しているんだよ。

わたしも
てつだうわ。

Girl: おおぜいでなにを
しているの？
What's going on with this big crowd?

Boy: あぁ、これはね。
Oh, I can explain.

Boy: 緑かうんどうで、緑をふやそうとこうえんで
ごみひろいやかだんのていれをしているんだ
よ。 It's a tree-planting campaign; we're picking up trash and repairing flower beds to keep the park green.

Girl: わたしもてつだうわ。 I'd like to help, then.

CAPITAL

都

みやこ、ツ、ト、

ex. 都合 (つごう) - circumstances
ex. 都会 (とかい) - city
ex. 都心 (としん) - center of the city

| 一 | 十 | 土 | 耂 | 耂 | 者 | 者 |
| 者 | 者 | 都 | 都 | | | |

ひっこしを
したんだって？

そうなんだ。

やちんの都ごうで
都しんからは
すこしはなれて
いるけど。

うん、うん。

すめば都って
ところかな。

それならよかった。

Woman: ひっこしをしたんだって？
I heard that you moved?
Man: そうなんだ。
Yep, sure did.

Man: やちんの都ごうで都しんからはすこしはなれているけど。 Because of the rent situation, though, it's a bit far from the center of the city.
Woman: うん、うん。 Right, right.
Man: すめば都ってところかな。 But now that it's home, it's starting to grow on me.
Woman: それならよかった。 Glad to hear it.

BUD/SPROUT

芽

め、ガ

ex. 麦芽 (ばくが) - malt

ex. 発芽 (はつが) - budding

ex. 芽生え (めばえ) - bud; sprout

やったぁ！
芽(め)がでてきたぞ！
いったいなにをかいているの？
はつ芽(が)かんさつにっきをつけているの。

Sister: やったぁ！芽がでてきたぞ！
All right! It's sprouting!

Brother: いったいなにをかいているの？
What in the world are you doing?

Sister: はつ芽かんさつにっきをつけているの。
I'm keeping a journal of this plant's growth.

DUTY

ヤク、エキ

ex. 市役所 (しやくしょ) - city hall
ex. 役者 (やくしゃ) - actor
ex. 役目 (やくめ) - duty

こんかいのミュージカルは
役しゃがみんな役にぴったりで
すてきだったなぁ・・・。

そうだね。

でも、あのこ役が
いちおしかも～。

わかる、わかる。

Fist girl: こんかいのミュージカルは役しゃがみんな役にぴったりですてきだったなぁ・・・。
It was so great how everyone in that musical was just right for their part...

Second girl: そうだね。Yeah, it sure was.

Fist girl: でも、あのこ役がいちおしかも～。
But my pick was probably that child actor.

Second girl: わかる、わかる。
I know what you mean.

HARMONY

やわ（らぐ）、やわ（らげる）、ワ

ex. 平和 （へいわ） - peace
ex. 和風 （わふう） - Japanese-style
ex. 和服 （わふく） - Japanese clothing

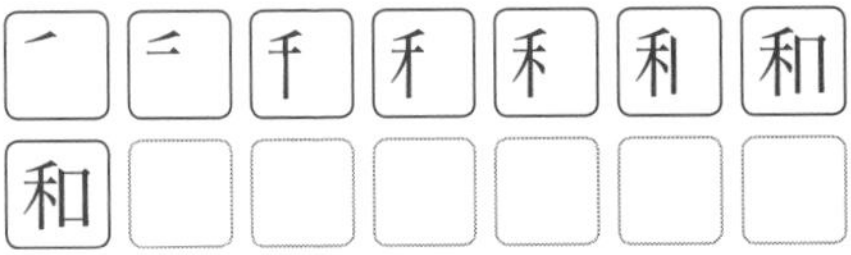

一 二 千 禾 禾 和 和 和

あのきものきている
ひと、にあっているし
びじん～！！

わたしも和ふくのにあう
じょせいを
めざそうかしら。

あ、
それいいね。

Girlfriend: あのきものきている
ひと、にあっているしびじん～！！
That woman over there wearing
a kimono, she looks so beautiful
in it!

Girlfriend: わたしも和ふくのにあうじょせいを
めざそうかしら。
I wonder how I would look if I tried to wear
Japanese clothes like that.

Boyfriend: あ、それいいね。
Oh, that would be great!

HOT WATER

ゆ、トウ

ex. お湯 (おゆ) - hot water
ex. 銭湯* (せんとう) - public bath
ex. 湯気 (ゆげ) - steam

あれ、
どこかにおでかけ？

あぁ、
じつはね…

すいどうがこわれて
お湯^ゆがでないから

これからせん湯^{とう}に
いくところなんだ。

それはたいへんね。

Girl: あれ、どこかにおでかけ？
Huh, are you going somewhere?

Boy: あぁ、じつはね・・・
Ah, well actually...

すいどうがこわれてお湯がでないからこれから
せん湯にいくところなんだ。
The plumbing is busted and I've got no hot water, so I'm on my way to the public bath.

Girl: それはたいへんね。
What a pain.

IN ADVANCE

ヨ

ex. 予習 (よしゅう) - preparation for a lesson
ex. 予想 (よそう) - prediction
ex. 予定 (よてい) - plan

㇇	マ	予	予			

なかなかべんきょうが
予ていどおりに
すすまないなぁ・・・。

ふくしゅうの
べんきょう？

それもあるけど・・・。

コキコキコキ

予しゅうもしなくちゃで
たいへんだよ～・・・。

がんばってね・・・。

Brother: なかなかべんきょうが
予ていどおりに
すすまないなぁ・・・。
Somehow I can never get
through my studies as
planned...
コキコキコキ (bones cracking)

Sister: ふくしゅうのべんきょう？Are you reviewing?

Brother: それもあるけど・・・。I have that too, but...
予しゅうもしなくちゃでたいへんだよ～・・・。
I've also gotta prepare for tomorrow's lesson;
it's just too much...

Sister: がんばってね・・・。Hang in there...

陽

SUNSHINE

ヨウ

ex. 陰と陽* (いんとよう) - yin and yang

ex. 太陽 (たいよう) - sun

ex. 陽気 (ようき) - season; weather

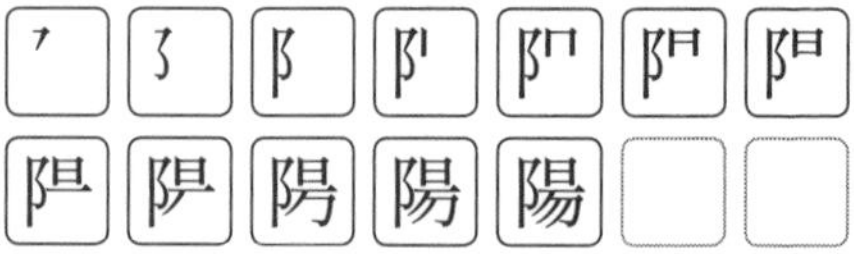

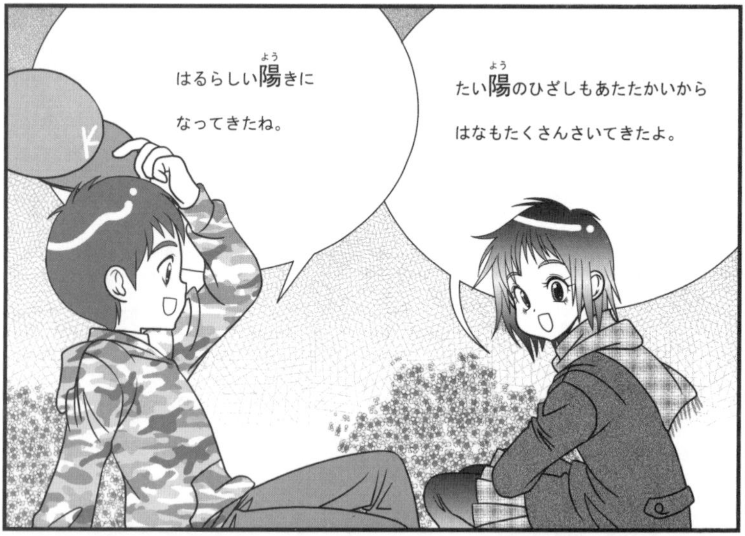
はるらしい陽(よう)きになってきたね。
たい陽(よう)のひざしもあたたかいからはなもたくさんさいてきたよ。

Boy: はるらしい陽きになってきたね。
The weather's gotten so nice, it's like springtime.

Girl: たい陽のひざしもあたたかいからはなもたくさんさいてきたよ。
The sunlight is warm too, so all the flowers are in bloom.

REASON

よし、ユ、ユイ、ユウ

ex. 経由 (けいゆ) - go by way of
ex. 自由 (じゆう) - freedom
ex. 由来 (ゆらい) - origin

由

Ｉ	冂	巾	由	由		

きょうのえんそくは
となりまちけい由で
もくてきちまでいきますよ。

り由は
あんぜんなみちを
とおるからです。

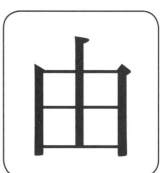

じ由じかんも
あるから、
がんばり
ましょうね。

Guide: きょうのえんそくはとなりまちけい由でもくてきちまでいきますよ。For today's hike we'll go by way of the next city to reach our destination.
Group: なぜですかー？
Why is that?

Guide: り由はあんぜんなみちをとおるからです。
The reason is so we can take a safer route.
Group: はーい OK!
Guide: じ由うじかんもあるから、がんばりましょうね。We've also got enough free time to do it, so let's do our best.
Group: はーい OK!

両

BOTH

リョウ

ex. 両替* (りょうがえ) - exchange (money)
ex. 両手 (りょうて) - both hands
ex. 両方 (りょうほう) - both

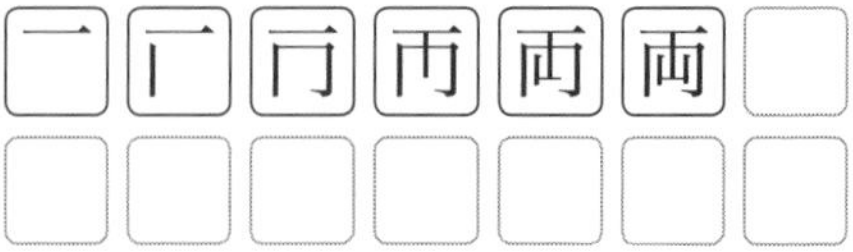

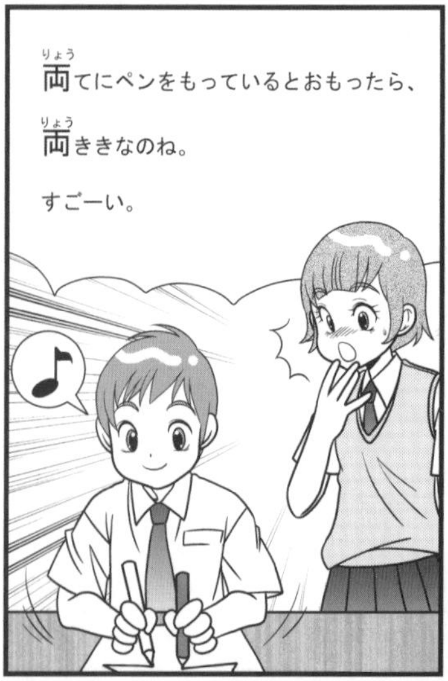
両てにペンをもっているとおもったら、
両ききなのね。
すごーい。

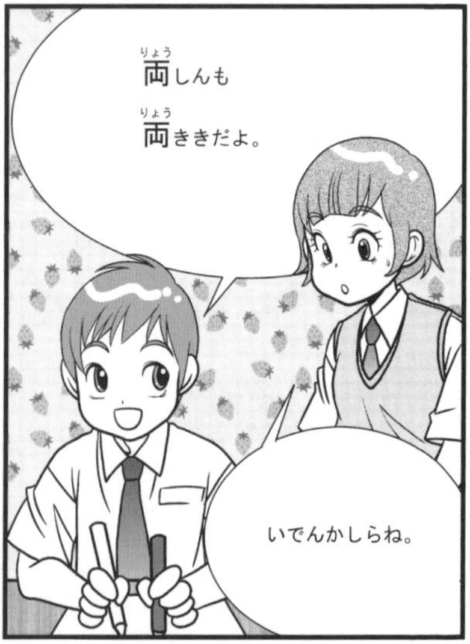
両しんも
両ききだよ。
いでんかしらね。

Schoolgirl: 両てにペンをもっているとおもったら、両ききなのね。すごーい。
I thought you were simply holding pens in each hand but you're actually ambidextrous, aren't you? That's amazing.

Schoolboy: 両しんも両ききだよ。
My parents are ambidextrous, too.

Schoolgirl: いでんかしらね。
Maybe it runs in the family.

GRATITUDE

レイ

礼

ex. お礼 (おれい) - expression of gratitude
ex. 礼儀* (れいぎ) - manners
ex. 礼服 (れいふく) - ceremonial dress

はい、
これおみやげ。
ありがとう
ございます。
しつれいします。
ぺこ
お礼もきちんといえて、
礼ぎただしいいい
おこさんね。
うんうん
ありがとう。

Aunt: はい、これおみやげ。
Here's your souvenir.

Nephew: ありがとうございます。
Thank you very much.
しつれいします。I'm truly honored.

ぺこ (a small bow)

Aunt: お礼もきちんといえて、
礼ぎただしいいいおこさんね。
He says "thank you" so properly and his manners are perfect; what a great kid.

うんうん (nodding in confirmation)

Boy's mom: ありがとう。Thanks.

列

ROW/LINE

レツ

ex. 整列 (せいれつ) - standing in a row
ex. 陳列* (ちんれつ) - display
ex. 配列 (はいれつ) - arrangement

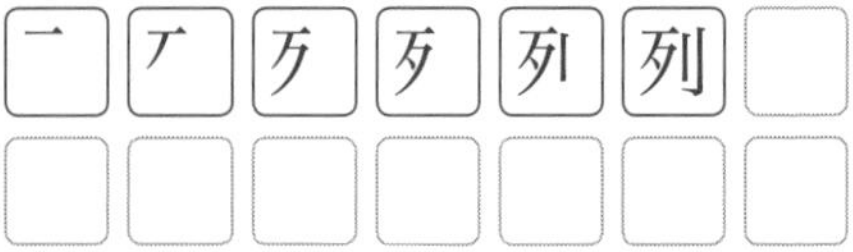

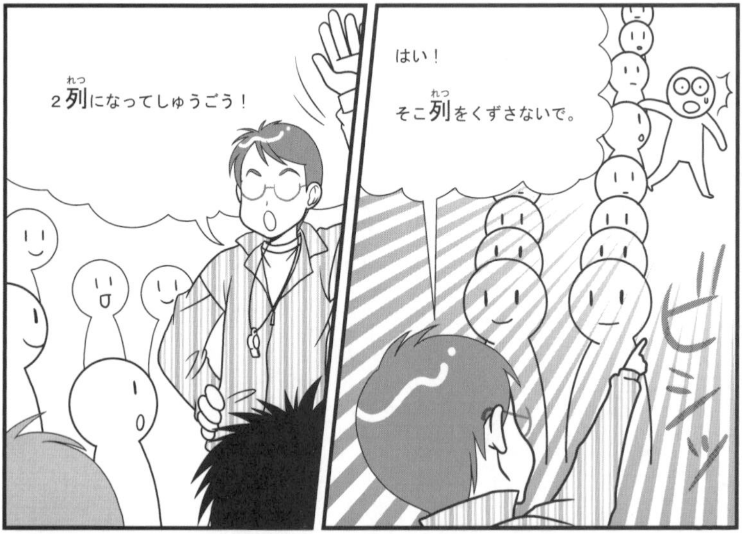
2列(れつ)になってしゅうごう！
はい！
そこ列(れつ)をくずさないで。
ビシッ

Coach: 2列になってしゅうごう!
Assemble into two single-file lines!

はい!そこ列をくずさないで。
OK! Don't break up the line there now.

ビシッ (suddenly pointing)

JUVENILE

わらべ、ドウ

ex. 童心 (どうしん) - child's mind
ex. 動揺* (どうよう) - nursery rhyme
ex. 童話 (どうわ) - fairy tale

わー。

この<ruby>童<rt>どう</rt></ruby>わなつかしい。

ほんとうだ。

よむとおもわず<ruby>童<rt>どう</rt></ruby>しんに

かえっちゃうわね・・・。

たまにはいいんじゃない？

First girl: わー。
この童わなつかしい。
Wow! This is such a nostalgic
fairy tale.

Second girl: ほんとうだ。
It sure is.

First girl: よむとおもわず童しんに
かえっちゃうわね・・・。
Reading it kind of makes you feel like a
kid again...

Second girl: たまにはいいんじゃない？
Isn't that nice every once in a while?

TAKE THE TEST

The Japanese Language Proficiency Test has been held annually throughout the world since 1984. Administered by the Japan Educational Exchanges and Services and the nonprofit Japan Foundation, the test evaluates and certifies the proficiency of non-native speakers of Japanese. There are four levels to the examination: Level 4 for beginners, Level 3 for intermediate students, Level 2 for those who are functionally literate in Japanese, and Level 1 for experts.

This book features 80 of the kanji students will need to know to pass Level 3 of the JLPT. Additional volumes in the award-winning *Kanji de Manga* series help students prepare for other levels.

For more information about the Japanese Language Proficiency Test, including examination locations in your country, please visit the JLPT website at http://www.jees.or.jp/jlpt/en/index.htm

Kanji de Manga

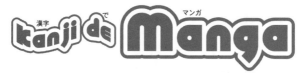

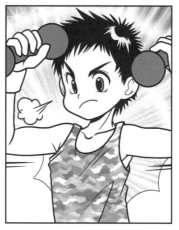

PRACTICE SECTION

KANJI INDEX

The 80 kanji featured in this volume of Kanji de Manga are indexed here based on their on-yomi and kun-yomi readings. This makes it easy to look up any kanji for which you know a pronunciation but cannot remember how the character is written. Because most kanji have more than one reading, you will find those characters listed multiple times in this index.

ALSO AVAILABLE FROM

MANGA UNIVERSITY

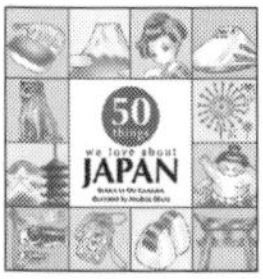
50
JAPAN

50 THINGS WE LOVE ABOUT JAPAN

By Edo Kurosawa & Atsuhisa Okura
ISBN-10: 4-921205-08-46 ISBN-13: 978-4-921205-08-9
Hardcover. English. 112 color pages. 5 inches x 5 inches.
US $9.99, CAN $11.99, UK £6.50

From *anime* to *karaoke* to *kaiten-zushi,* Nihon is number one when it comes to things that are cool. This fun little book features cute manga illustrations and delightful prose to offer the rest of the world a glimpse at what the Japanese love most about the country they call home.

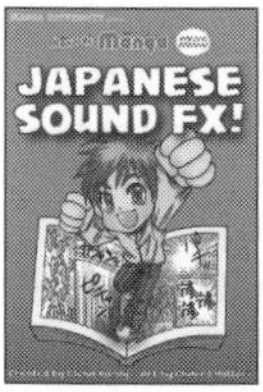
JAPANESE
SOUND FX!

KANA DE MANGA SPECIAL EDITION
Japanese Sound FX!

By Glenn Kardy & Chihiro Hattori
ISBN 4-921205-12-4
Paperback. English. 112 b/w pages. 5 inches x 7 inches.
US $9.99, CAN $11.99, UK £6.50

Onomatopoeia fill the pages of authentic manga. Written in hiragana and katakana, they are just as important to the story as the dialogue and drawings. This special edition of *Kana de Manga* uses all-new artwork to show Japanese onomatopoiea in action—and explain what they mean.

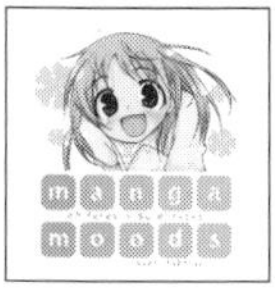
manga
moods

MANGA MOODS
40 Faces + 80 Phrases

By Saori Takarai
ISBN-10: 4-921205-13-2 ISBN-13: 978-4-921205-13-3
Hardcover. English. 96 color pages. 5 inches x 5 inches.
US $9.99, CAN $11.99, UK £6.50

Do you have mood swings? Well, you're not alone! The kawaii (that's Japanese for "cute") characters in *Manga Moods* know exactly how you feel! Whether they're giddy or grumpy, or something in between, these cuties always manage to put on their best faces. And while they're at it, they'll teach you how to speak a little Japanese, too.

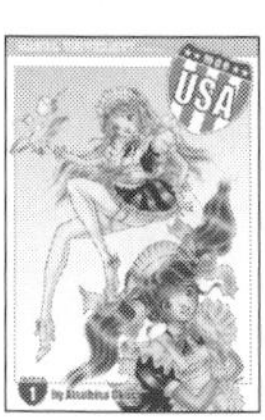
USA

MOE USA
Volume 1: Maid in Japan

By Atsuhisa Okura
ISBN-10: 4-921205-19-1 ISBN-13: 978-4-921205-19-5
Paperback. English. 160 b/w pages. 5 inches x 7 inches.
US $9.99, CAN $11.99, UK £6.50

Moe USA chronicles the antics of two all-American girls who land jobs as waitresses in a Tokyo maid cafe. Despite their "moe" (pronounced "moh-ay," Japanese slang for "super-cute") appeal, the girls seem destined for failure. That is, until they discover a couple of magical maid costumes that change their lives forever!

GLENN KARDY is director of Japanime, an award-winning creative agency and publisher of Manga University's acclaimed lineup of educational materials. He lives in the Tokyo suburb of Kawaguchi City with his wife, their daughter and a collection of Oakland A's bobblehead dolls.

CHIHIRO HATTORI has been the featured artist in all nine volumes of the *Kana de Manga/Kanji de Manga* series, and she also illustrated Manga University's *Manga Cookbook*. Chihiro, her husband and their son live in Yokohama, where they enjoy fine food, fast cars and high fashion.

Cover illustrations by Chihiro Hattori
Introduction by Edward Mazza
Art coordinator: Mari Oyama
Translator: Naomi Rubin
Sales director: Chris Kardy
Editorial assistant: Tom Nucci